LAIRD & LEE'S

GUIDE TO

Historic Virginia

AND THE

Jamestown Centennial

Originally Published in 1907 for the
Jamestown Tercentennial Celebration

2007 Jamestown Quadricentennial
Commemorative Edition

First Printing
Copyright © 2006 The Vision Forum, Inc.
All Rights Reserved

"Where there is no vision, the people perish." (Proverbs 29:18)

The Vision Forum, Inc.
4719 Blanco Rd., San Antonio, Texas 78212
www.visionforum.com

ISBN-10 0-9787559-4-4
ISBN-13 978-0-9787559-4-2

En Dat Virginium Quintam

Printed in the United States of America

LAIRD & LEE'S

GUIDE TO

Historic Virginia

AND THE

Jamestown Centennial

The Historic Sights of the Old Dominion Graphically and
Realistically Portrayed with Authentic Descriptions of
the Important Events and Associations that Have
Made Famous Jamestown, Williamsburg, York-
town, Smithfield, Norfolk, Hampton, Newport
News, Old Point Comfort, Fortress Monroe,
Portsmouth, Virginia Beach, Cape Henry,
Petersburg, Richmond and the Noted Bat-
tlefields of the Civil War. Full Statistics
and Itinerary. Also Concise Directions
for Visiting These Many Famous
Places with the Greatest Possible
Saving of Time and Expense.

BEAUTIFULLY ILLUSTRATED
BY
NUMEROUS HALFTONES, MAPS and DIAGRAMS

Copyright, 1907, by Wm. H. Lee

CHICAGO, U. S. A.
LAIRD & LEE, Publishers

———

This historic reprint is dedicated to three generations of defenders of the Jamestown legacy:

President John Tyler,
Lyon Gardiner Tyler, LL.D., and
Harrison Tyler

PUBLISHER'S INTRODUCTION.

"Remove not the ancient landmark."
(Proverbs 22:28)

There are two great landmarks to the dawn of American liberty. The first is Jamestown and the second is Plymouth. Both were birthed out of evangelical zeal to see the spread of Christianity. Both involved intrepid men who risked much for the hope of blessing and prosperity for generations yet to be born. Of the two, Jamestown was the first. To the legacy of Jamestown, Americans owe many of their most noteworthy principles of self-government and freedom.

Her founding in 1607 resulted in the introduction and establishment in North America of the ancient Christian common law, with its origins in the Law of Moses and the Magna Charta. This common law would later be incorporated by direct reference into the United States Constitution. To Jamestown, we owe America's first great experiment in republican representative government, a model that would later be adopted by the Founding Fathers as the basic construct of civil government in a free society. Jamestown gave the American people their first Protestant Christian worship services, church buildings, and baptisms. America's first interracial marriage took place in Jamestown between America's first baptized, Christian convert, Pocahontas, and a devout tobacco farmer named John Rolfe. Their progeny live on to this very day.

For the past two hundred years, Americans have used the anniversaries of the founding of Jamestown to communicate gratitude and respect for the remarkable legacy of liberty purchased by our colonial forefathers. For the bicentennial of 1807, Americans met in Jamestown and Williamsburg for a five-day celebration which included "a regatta of sailing vessels, a tent bazaar, a parade, the recitation of odes and orations by the students of the College of William and Mary, and an *al fresco* banquet followed by dancing at nearby plantations."[1]

Nearly eight thousand people journeyed to Jamestown for the 250th celebration in 1857. The featured speaker on that occasion was the tenth president of the United States and the owner of nearby Sherwood Forest, John Tyler.

Remarkably, President Tyler's grandson, Harrison Tyler, is the present owner of his grandfather's Sherwood Forest estate. He is perhaps the only grandson in America who can claim, as he once did to me: "if my grandfather were alive today, he would be more than 215 years old." Notably, Harrison Tyler's father, Lyon Gardiner Tyler (the son of the tenth president), served as president of the College of William and Mary during the tercentennial celebration of 1907. He remains among the most noteworthy Jamestown historians of all time. His book, *Narratives of Early Virginia*, published in the tercentennial year, remains an outstanding primary source of information on the Jamestown founding of America.

The Jamestown Exposition of 1907 was massive in scope. It attracted millions including foreign

---

1   The 350th Anniversary of Jamestown, 1607-1957; Final Report to the President and Congress of the Jamestown-Williamsburg-Yorktown Celebration Commission, 1959, pg. 4.

dignitaries and great personages like Theodore Roosevelt and Samuel Clemons (a.k.a. Mark Twain), both of whom addressed audiences in attendance for the festivities.

It was for the occasion of the great 1907 Jamestown Exposition that Laird & Lee published the guide in your hands. For the four hundredth anniversary of the Jamestown settlement, Vision Forum has reproduced this guide in its entirety. Frankly, it is remarkable to see how many things have remained relatively untouched over the last century. There have been a number of improvements, preservations, and historical markers erected since the tercentennial, but the most ancient of America's colonial landmarks seems surprisingly locked in time—an unchanging, visual testimony of perseverance to a nation which for four hundred years has been the recipient of unprecedented blessings and providential kindness.

Persevero,
Douglas W. Phillips, Esq.
College of William and Mary, '87
Publisher

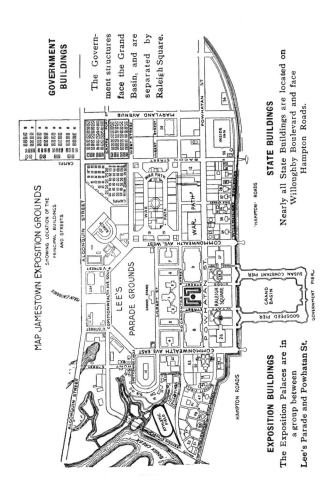

GOVERNMENT BUILDINGS

The Government structures face the Grand Basin, and are separated by Raleigh Square.

STATE BUILDINGS

Nearly all State Buildings are located on Willoughby Boulevard and face Hampton Roads.

EXPOSITION BUILDINGS

The Exposition Palaces are in a group between Lee's Parade and Powhatan St.

MAP JAMESTOWN EXPOSITION GROUNDS
SHOWING LOCATION OF THE
PRINCIPAL BUILDINGS
AND STREETS

QUICK REFERENCE INDEX

OFFICIAL PENNANT,

JAMESTOWN EXPOSITION.

LIST OF ILLUSTRATIONS

PAGE

MAP OF VIRGINIA

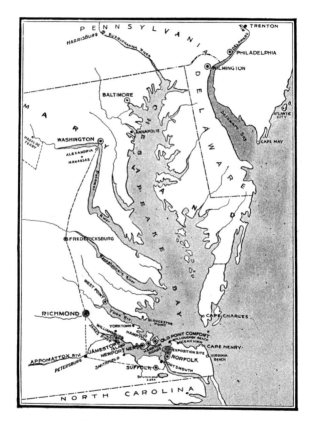

**SHOWING PRINCIPAL CITIES AND HISTORICAL
PLACES OF INTEREST**

THE DAWN OF AMERICAN HISTORY.

Few people realize that the Cradle of the Republic was not the rock-bound coasts of New England, but the rich valleys of Virginia. Upon her fertile fields, the armies of three wars bivouacked, and as early as 1765 the fires of patriotism were kindled in the House of Burgesses at Williamsburg. Since the days of Patrick Henry, the state has given birth to many illustrious men; patriots whose fame has shaken the thrones of the Old World and revolutionized the customs and usages of the New Republic.

Many who visit Tidewater Virginia for the first time express the utmost astonishment on learning that nothing remains of historic Jamestown but a few crumbling ruins on an uninhabited island, nearly forty miles up the James River from Norfolk and the site of the Jamestown Exposition.

In the blood stained soil of the Old Dominion lie buried the ancestry and chivalry of our Nation, and no patriotic American should neglect to visit the sacred shrines that have become interwoven with the very warp and woof of our national history. Any one making the itinerary laid out in these chapters, cannot fail to become imbued with admiration for the sturdy colonists who made the wilderness to blossom as the rose; out of primeval forests erecting the sturdy foundations of our glorious Ship of State.

After each hallowed spot has been seen, the tourist will appreciate the real spirit that has made pos-

sible the commemoration of the three hundredth anniversary of the first settlement in America of English speaking people.

From the sturdy little band of pilgrims who landed
at Jamestown three hundred years ago have come
the spirit and the courage, the zeal and the energy
which have conquered the powers of Europe, chained
the lightning's flash and harnessed the mighty tor-
rents of Niagara.

Here began our history; from out of this deserted
island, a mighty nation came into existence and, in
the ivy-clad churchyards of Virginia, quietly sleep
the statesmen, warriors and presidents, who with
others, were directly responsible for American Independence. In the midst of these historic associations,
every citizen should be proud to uncover, and rever-
ently say, "Thank God, I am an American."

TYPE OF MONITOR USED IN THE CIVIL WAR.

CHAPTER I.

Three hundred years ago, the thirteenth of May, 1607, the foundation of the American Republic was laid by a sturdy band of English explorers at Jamestown, now desolate and deserted.

Prior to 1607, Spain had gained a successful foothold in the New World. The defeat of the Spanish Armada awakened England's desire to push her conquests westward. A charter for the colonization of Virginia was granted to Sir Walter Raleigh in 1584, and Amadas and Barlowe were sent to explore the coast and chart the rivers. Upon their return, Raleigh sent out a party of colonists under Sir Ralph Lane. For a year they remained in America, where many died from fever, while others were killed by Indians. In 1586, the remainder were brought back to England by Sir Francis Drake. Two other expeditions were sent out but failed. In 1602, Gosnold surveyed the coast of New England and called it North Virginia. No settlement, however, was made.

December 20, 1606, an expedition started for the New World under command of Capt. Christopher Newport. Among the passengers was one John Smith, destined to play an important part in the colony to be founded. Three boats constituted the entire outfit: The "Susan Constance," the "Discovery," under John Ratcliffe, and the "Godspeed," under Bartholomew Gosnold. Their destination was the island of Roanoke, but after four months of sailing, on April

26, 1607, they were driven by a fierce gale into the Chesapeake. The southern cape they named Henry and the northern Charles, in honor of the sons of King James. At Cape Henry, the savages drove them back to their ships and the little band proceeded to Hampton Roads, anchoring at a sheltered place which they named Point Comfort.

TABLET ON CAPE
HENRY LIGHTHOUSE

A few days later they sailed up the James River, then called Powhatan, anchoring May 13, off a peninsula, thirty-five miles from the mouth of the James. Having landed, the first thing they did was to erect a tent in which to hold religious services, and here, under Rev. Robert Hunt, began the first English Church in America.

Newport soon returned to England for more provisions and new colonists, leaving one hundred and five settlers alone in the wilderness. Capt. John Smith had been appointed one of the magistrates by the London Company, but during the voyage jealousy arose and he was accused of designing to usurp the provincial government and make himself king of Virginia. He was arrested and confined during the voyage, but liberated on their arrival when he demanded a trial. He was finally acquitted and took his place in the council.

Ravaged by fever and sickness, attacked by savages and torn by internal dissention, the colony was only held together by the indomitable spirit of Smith. As many as four or five died every day, among them the intrepid explorer, Gosnold. Upon Newport's return from England only thirty-eight of the original one hundred and five settlers remained.

In an attempt to explore the head waters of the Chickahominy, Smith was attacked and captured by Indians. By showing them his compass he managed to divert their attention until he was led in triumph before Powhatan, their chief. The Council finally condemned him to death, but as the savages circled around him in silence with Powhatan ready to strike the fatal blow, Pocahontas pushed herself to the side of the prisoner and dramatically threw herself between him and his captors.

CAPT. JOHN SMITH

Through her intercession, the life of Smith was saved and the next morning he was conducted back to Jamestown, seven weeks after his capture. This exciting incident is described by Capt. Smith himself in the following language:

"A long consultation was held, the conclusion of which was that two great stones were brought before Powhatan. As many as could laid hands on him, dragged him to them, and thereon laid his head; and being ready with their clubs to beat out his brains, Pocahontas, the King's dearest daughter, when no entreaty could prevail, got his head on her arms, laid her own upon his to save him from death; whereat the Emperor was content he should live to make him hatchets, beads and copper.''

POCAHONTAS

In 1609, Powhatan plotted to destroy Jamestown, but through Pocahontas, his daughter, the colonists were warned in time to protect themselves. Subsequently Pocahontas was baptized by the name of Rebecca. She married Rolfe, with whom she visited England, where she died, leaving one son. It has been said she was in love with Capt. Smith, who was many years her senior and whom she after met in England.

When Smith left for England, the Colony numbered five hundred, but famine and pestilence besieged the hardy pioneers and in May, 1610, only sixty disheartened, haggard settlers remained. June 7, 1610, with the drums rolling a dirge, the few dejected colonists set sail for England, arriving at Hampton Roads in time to meet the ships of Lord Delaware, the new governor, who had just arrived with a supply of provisions and one hundred and eighty new adventurers who put new hope into their hearts.

From this time the Colony prospered. In 1619, in the wooden church at Jamestown, Gov. Yeardly convened the first legislative assembly in Virginia, the upper house being called the Council and the lower one the House of Burgesses.

March 22, 1622, three hundred and forty-seven of the colony were butchered by the Indians. In 1624, the Crown took over the government of the colony, dissolving the charter of the London Company. Up to this time nine thousand colonists had been sent to Virginia, but only two thousand had survived. Grants conveyed by the London Company were taken away and settlers deprived of their lawful holdings; agents sent to England to remedy the wrong, returned unsuccessful and after years of abuse at the hands of the king, discontent culminated in open insurrection under the leadership of Nathaniel Bacon.

Governor Berkeley refused to dispatch forces against the Susquehannah Indians, who were on the war path; but in 1676 Bacon for this purpose raised six hundred volunteers, who were denounced by the Governor as rebels.

Civil war now ensued and Jamestown was burned by Bacon's men. The death of Bacon became the end of the rebellion and Berkeley eventually returned to England, where he died.

After Bacon's death, Berkeley hung all of those who had opposed him upon whom he could lay hands. The wife of Major Chessman begged the old governor upon her knees to spare her husband, but without avail. Even his old-time friend, William Drummond, was sacrificed to his wrath.

"Mr. Drummond," he said in a sneering voice, "you are very welcome! I am more glad to see you than any man in Virginia! Mr. Drummond, you shall be hanged in half an hour!''

As soon as King Charles II heard of this he restored to Mrs. Drummond her husband's property which the governor had confiscated.

''That old fool,'' said Charles II, ''has hanged more men in that naked country than I did for the murder of my father!''

Owing to the fever, which seemed prevalent so much of the time, it was decided to abandon the site at Jamestown and remove the seat of government to Williamsburg, which was done in 1699, the year after the burning of the State-House.

The waters of the James River have long since converted the peninsula into an island. Fire and sword, pestilence and famine have done their work, and only ruins remain to mark the site of historic old Jamestown, but the struggles and sufferings of the early colonists were not unavailing, for after Jamestown came Williamsburg, which first fanned the flames of the Revolution leading to the glorious victory at Yorktown and the subsequent birth of the American Republic.

CHAPTER II.

BATTLESHIPS ON HAMPTON ROADS

Certainly, the most historic body of water in the United States, Hampton Roads, is also, perhaps, the most beautiful harbor on the Atlantic coast. In shape, it is an isosceles triangle, eleven miles long on one side and nine miles in length on the other two sides, forming an area of about fifty square miles, sheltered by the Virginia coasts, connecting Chesapeake Bay with the Atlantic Ocean. Into this vast body of water flow the Elizabeth, Nansemond and James Rivers, the latter being four miles wide at its mouth.

A glance at the bird's-eye view on page 20 will show the exact location of these streams, with the cities bordering the shores of the Roads. The waters are deep enough for the largest war vessels built and extensive enough to manoeuvre the largest fleet afloat. Sheltered by Cape Henry and Cape Charles, Willoughby Spit and Old Point; provided with one of the largest ship building plants and dry docks in the world and supplied by one of the most important government

Navy Yards, Hampton Roads has long been considered the strategic naval center of the Atlantic coast.

In the days of the early discoveries, it became the objective point of the storm-driven colonists. Almost the first guns discharged by the British navy at the commencement of the Revolutionary War were fired by Lord Dunmore upon Norfolk and the cities of Hampton Roads. In 1779 the British again invaded Hampton Roads, capturing Portsmouth and the navy yard, and the French admirals, D'Estaing and De Grasse, later sailed to Washington's aid at Yorktown through these historic waters.

When after the battle of Waterloo, the portentous events of the period prevented Napoleon from remaining in Paris, it was planned that he should escape to Hampton Roads. However, an attorney at Bordeaux persuaded him against this course and he put to sea from Rochefort and was soon captured by the British frigate Bellerophon. His brother, though, refused to follow the attorney's advice and reached America in safety. Prince Louis Bonaparte, Napoleon's nephew and later Emperor of France, sixteen years after, sailed into Hampton Roads with the French frigates L'Andromede and La Sirene on a visit to Norfolk.

In the War of 1812, naval activities again centered around Hampton Roads. June 22, 1813, preparatory to entering Norfolk, the British attacked Craney Island, at the mouth of the Elizabeth River. As they passed Nansemond Point, they were discovered and attacked by a battery on the shore manned by marines from the Constellation. Three barges were sunk and most of the men drowned, the few survivors retreating to their vessels. Those who had previously landed were repulsed by the Virginia militia.

During the Civil War, Hampton Roads became an important strategic point, as it was the gateway to Washington. Here, almost opposite the site of the Jamestown Exposition, the Monitor and the Merrimac fought their epoch-making battle, and over its waters thundered the guns of Fortress Monroe and the battleships of both navies.

THE ESSEX, AN OLD-TIME WARSHIP.

What Yorktown or Gettysburg have been to our land forces, Hampton Roads has been our navy. Protected by Fortress Monroe and the Rip Raps, it is the gateway to our shores; the harbor for every storm-beaten mariner and the defender against every invading foreign foe.

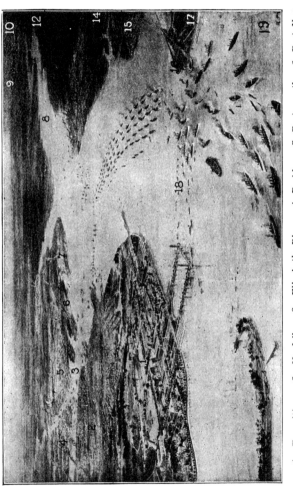

1, Exposition. 2, Norfolk. 3, Elizabeth River. 4, Berkley. 5, Portsmouth. 6, Port Norfolk. 7, West Norfolk. 8, James River. 9, Petersburg. 10, Richmond. 11, Jamestown Island. 12, Williamsburg. 13, Newport News. 14, Hampton. 15, Phoebus. 16, Old Point Comfort. 17, Fortress Monroe. 18, Location Monitor and Merrimac Battle. 19, Atlantic Ocean.

CHAPTER III.

Norfolk is the headquarters of nearly all visitors to tidewater Virginia. The city has many good hotels, the principal ones being the Monticello, on Granby Street, Monticello and City Hall Avenues; the Lorraine, Granby and Tazewell Streets; the Atlantic and the Fairfax.

Having secured a location, the tourist should study the relative position of Norfolk and other tidewater cities of Virginia. The bird's-eye view given on page 20 conveys an accurate idea of the contiguous territory. As seen from this map, Norfolk is situated on the north side of the Elizabeth River at the mouth of its eastern branch, opposite Berkley and Portsmouth. This river and its branches are arms of Chesapeake Bay, forming a harbor of about 1,000 acres, thirty feet deep, connecting with Hampton Roads, an outer harbor of forty or fifty square miles.

On this body of water is located the site of the Jamestown Exposition, opposite Fortress Monroe, Old Point, Hampton and Newport News, and into Hampton Roads flow the waters of the James River. As a matter of reference a few statistics regarding Norfolk may not be out of place.

In 1905, the city had 136 miles of electric roads, 14 hospitals and asylums, 14 newspapers, 12 hotels, 9 places of amusement, 7 railroad lines, 22 steamship lines, 14 banks, 92 benevolent orders, 18 schools, 76 churches, 125 miles of paved, curbed and graded streets, 50 miles of sewers, 5 city buildings, 3 libraries and 6 public parks.

In addition to being a great railway and steam boat terminus, Norfolk is an important manufacturing center. In 1900 nearly seven hundred manufacturing establishments were reported, with an aggregate capital of nearly eighteen million dollars. Lumber, cotton, peanuts, wines, oysters, fish and fertilizers are the principal products handled. Truck farming and ship building are also important industries.

The principal business streets of Norfolk are Main, Granby and Church Streets. Having strolled through the business sections, the tourist can spend a short time in visiting the more important places of interest, but before doing this, a short synopsis of the city's history may be read with profit.

Prior to the settlement of the English in the state, Eastern Virginia was occupied by forty different Indian tribes, thirty of them belonging to Powhatan's Confederacy.

> "Alas, for them! their day is o'er;
> Their fires are out, from shore to shore;
> No more for them the wild deer bounds,
> The plough is on their hunting grounds."

In 1662, two hundred acres of land now occupied by the city was owned by Lewis Vandermull, who sold it to a shipwright named Nicholas Wise, Sen. In 1680, fifty acres of this land was purchased for a townsite for "Tenn thousand pounds of tobacco and Caske." Sept. 15, 1736, the town was incorporated as a Royal Borough and Sam'l Boush became the first mayor.

The name Norfolk, pronounced Norfolke, was given

NORFOLK CITY MACE

to the county by Colonel Thorogood in memory of his native county in England. Many of the streets were named in honor of early settlers, Colonial governors and officials, as Dunmore, Botetourt and Washington.

The accompanying illustration shows the original Norfolk mace presented to the corporation by Robert Dinwiddie, Lieut. Governor of Virginia, 1753. It is 40½ inches long and is surmounted by an arched crown with orb and cross, with the Royal Arms engraved beneath the crown. It was hidden in a bank vault during the Civil War and thus kept intact from designing hands.

Up to 1776 Norfolk continued to grow and prosper, but with the commencement of the Revolutionary War her troubles began. The most interesting evidence of these troublous times is the old church, with its cannon-ball.

Old St. Paul's Church (Church Street).—Elizabeth River Parish was established 1637 and the first church erected at ''Sewell's Point.'' The first Norfolk church was built 1641, but no trace of it can be found. The present edifice was erected in 1739 and became known as the ''Borough Church.''

OLD ST. PAUL'S CHURCH, NORFOLK

The site was presented to the Parish by Sam'l Boush, the first mayor of Norfolk, and his initials can still be seen on a brick in the south wing. He is buried in the old churchyard. Rev. John Wilson was the first rector. In 1761 the parish was divided into Elizabeth River, Portsmouth and St. Bride's parishes.

After Lord Dunmore's defeat Dec. 2, 1775, at Great Bridge, ten miles from Norfolk, he retired to his fleet in Norfolk harbor. Jan. 1, 1776, he began bombarding Norfolk, destroying a goodly portion of the town.

A 5½ inch cannon-ball struck the south wall of Old St. Paul's under the eaves near the Church street corner. The ball fell to the ground and in 1848 it was found and dug up by Capt. Seabury and cemented into the cavity it made in the church wall.

In 1901 the Great Bridge Chapter, Daughters of the American Revolution, erected a tablet on the wall, which reads, "Fired by Lord Dunmore, Jan. 1, 1776." The church was disestablished as a result of the Revolutionary War and its glebe lands were confiscated by the state.

In 1832 it was repaired and consecrated as St. Paul's. During the Civil War, it was occupied by Federal troops from 1862 to 1865. For damage done the church during the war, the government has since awarded $3,600. It was repaired and the interior restored in 1892 and the tower erected 1901.

Churchyard (Nearly Two Acres in Extent).—Over 265 tombs are recorded in the records of St. Paul's. The inscriptions have been copied and indexed in a book. The oldest date is Jan. 18, 1673, on the stone marking the grave of "Dorothy Farrell." Another stone, not marking any grave, was brought from King's Creek and bears an inscription to the memory of Elizabeth, wife of Honorable Nathaniel Bacon. Dr. Okeson, who was responsible for the restoration of the church after the Civil War, was buried in the churchyard by special permission from the city.

One of the queer epitaphs reads:

> "Behold my grave, how low I lie!
> As you are now, so once was I.
> As I am now, so you must be,
> Then be prepared to follow me."

It is said that during the Civil War a soldier was responsible for scratching on the tomb, with his saber, the additional lines:

"To follow you I am not bent
Until I know which way you went."

Jóhn Hancock's Chair.—In the vestry-room of St.
Paul's is a mahogany arm chair, upholstered in leather
bearing a silver plate with the following inscription:

"This chair was occupied by John Hancock when
he signed the Declaration of Independence. It
was bought by Colonel Thomas M. Bayley, of
Accomac County, Virginia. At his death it became
the property of his daughter Ann, who subsequently intermarried with the Rev. Benjamin M.
Miller, once rector of St. Paul's Church, Norfolk,
Va., who presented it to the parish."

Norfolk Academy (Bank and Charlotte Street).—
Incorporated Jan. 15, 1804. Present building erected
1840; a gem of architectural beauty, modeled after
the Temple of Theseus at Athens. Prior to the Revolution the site belonged to St. Paul's Church. This
building was the edifice in which Poe, the famous
American poet, delivered his last lecture.

Thomas Moore's House (End of East Main Street).

A deserted dormer-windowed house, where the Irish
poet is said to have lived. While in Norfolk, it is
claimed that Moore wrote the first part of ''Lalla
Rookh'' and the poem associated with Lake Drummond in the middle of the Dismal Swamp.

It is said a young man who had lost his mind upon
the death of his sweetheart had suddenly disappeared
and was never heard of afterwards. In his ravings
he declared firmly that the girl was not dead but had
gone to the Dismal Swamp. Upon this supposition, it
was believed that the young man had wandered into
this wilderness and had starved to death among the
morasses of the Swamp. Upon this story, Moore based
his poem, given as follows:

The Lake of the Dismal Swamp.

"They made her a grave too cold and damp
  For a soul so warm and true;
And she's gone to the lake of the Dismal Swamp,
Where all night long, by a fire-fly lamp,
  She paddles her white canoe.

"And her fire-fly lamp I soon shall see,
  And her paddle I soon shall hear;
Long and loving our life shall be,
And I'll hide the maid in a cypress tree,
  When the footstep of death is near!"

Away to the Dismal Swamp he speeds;
  His path was rugged and sore;
Through tangled juniper, beds of reeds,
Through many a fen, where the serpent feeds,
  And man never trod before.

And when on the earth he sank to sleep,
  If slumber his eyelids knew,
He lay where the deadly vine doth weep
Its venomous tear and nightly steep,
  The flesh with blistering dew!

And near him the she-wolf stirred the brake,
  And the coppersnake breathed in his ear,
Till he starting cried, from his dream awake,
"Oh! when shall I see the dusty lake,
  And the white canoe of my dear!"

He saw the lake and the meteor bright
  Quick over its surface played—
"Welcome!" he said; "my dear one's light!"
And the dim shore echoed for many a night,
  The name of the death-cold maid.

Till he hollowed a boat of the birchen bark,
  Which carried him off from shore;
Far he followed the meteor spark;
The wind was high and the clouds were dark,
  And the boat returned no more.

But oft from the Indian hunter's camp,
  This lover and maid so true,
Are seen at the hour of midnight damp,
To cross the lake by a fire-fly lamp,
  And paddle their white canoe.

The Dismal Swamp covers an area of 800 or 1,000 square miles. Before the war attempts were made to reclaim it, and within the last few years much has been established here, one containing 4,000 acres and another 1,000 acres. The soil is the richest and most productive in the world.

A canal traverses the eastern part of it, connecting Chesapeake Bay with the sounds of North Carolina. Near the center, three miles west of the canal, is Lake Drummond, 18 miles from Norfolk. It is estimated that the entire swamp could be reclaimed at an expense of $4,000,000, in which case an annual revenue could be obtained from the timber amounting to $100,-000 and at least $2,000,000 from agricultural products. A splendid place for hunting and fishing.

Edgar Allan Poe spent the greater part of his life in Virginia and frequently visited Norfolk. He was a student at the University of Virginia in 1826. Sept. 18, 1849, he wrote from Richmond to his mother-in-law, as follows:

"I lectured at Norfolk on Monday and cleared enough to settle my bill here at the Madison House, with $2 over. I had a highly fashionable audience, but Norfolk is a small place and there were two exhibitions the same night."

Sept. 13, 1849, the Norfolk Argus published his now well known poem, ''Lenore,'' appended herewith:

Lenore.

Ah, broken is the golden bowl! the spirit flown forever!
Let the bell toll!—a saintly soul floats on the Stygian river;
And, Guy De Vere, hast *thou* no tear!—weep now or never
    more!
See! on yon drear and rigid bier low lies thy love, Lenore!
Come! let the burial rite be read—the funeral song be
    sung!—
An anthem for the queenliest dead that ever died so young—
A dirge for her the doubly dead in that she died so young.

"Wretches! ye loved her for her wealth and hated her for
    her pride,
"And when she fell in feeble health, ye blessed her—that
    she died!
"How *shall* the ritual, then, be read! the requiem how be
    sung
"By you—by yours, the evil eye—by yours, the slanderous
    tongue

"That did to death the innocence that died, and died so
    young!"

Peccavimus! but rave not thus! and let a Sabbath song
Go up to God so solemnly that dead may feel no wrong!
The sweet Lenore hath "gone before" with Hope, that flew
    beside,
Leaving thee wild for the dear child that should have been
    thy bride—
For her, the fair and debonair, that now so lowly lies,
The life upon her yellow hair but not within her eyes—
The life still there, upon her hair—the death upon her eyes.

"Avaunt! tonight my heart is light. No dirge will I up-
    raise,
"But waft the angel on her flight with a Paean of old days!
"Let *no* bell toll!—lest her sweet soul, mid its hallowed
    mirth,
"Should catch the note, as it doth float up from the damned
    Earth.
"To friends above, from friends below, the indignant ghost
    is riven—
"From Hell unto a high estate far up within the Heaven—
"From grief and groan, to a golden throne, beside the King
    of Heaven."

Another famous visitor to Norfolk was General
Lafayette, who with George Washington, received a
public ovation here in 1824. In 1837 Louis Napoleon
Bonaparte, subsequently Emperor of France, was entertained at French's Hotel, Main and Church streets,
and in 1844 Henry Clay visited the city.

In 1855 yellow fever frightfully devastated Norfolk,
St. Paul's Church alone furnishing seventy-six vic-
tims. St. Mary's Church was converted into a tem-
porary hospital. This edifice still stands, one of the
most beautiful churches in the south, a monument to
the faithful priest, who during this awful scourge
ministered to the sick and dying.

The Civil War proved still another factor that inter-
fered with the growth of the city.

Confederate Monument.—At the intersection of Main
Street and Commercial Place. This statue commemo-
rates the memory of the Confederate Soldiers who died
for the "lost cause."

The points of interest at surrounding towns are fully described in separate chapters, and directions for reaching these places will be found in the "Itinerary," Part III. There are many historical places of interest within an hour's ride of Norfolk, which every tourist should visit. The cars going to the various suburbs of Norfolk are given as follows:

Ghent.—The west end residence district. To see this part of the city, take City Park and Atlantic City cars, or the City Park, Ghent and Lambert's Point cars.

Brambleton.—East end residence district. Take east-bound Brambleton, Norfolk and Western, and Norfolk and Southern cars.

Edgewater.—Take west-bound Lambert's Point cars which leave City Parks.

Berkley.—Take cars on City Hall Avenue, near Granby Street, or Ferry at foot of Commercial Place.

Portsmouth.—Take Ferry, foot of Commercial Place.

Norfolk Navy Yard and Marine Hospital.—Take Ferry to Portsmouth and electric car to the yards.

Exposition Grounds.—Take electric cars at barn.

CHAPTER IV.

Portsmouth is only a few minutes' ride across the Elizabeth River. The principal attractions to be seen are the Norfolk Navy Yards, Trinity Church and the Confederate Monument. The business of the city is largely dependent upon the industries represented by the Navy Yard. Many residents are also employed in Norfolk and surrounding places.

History records the fact that Ralph Lane landed near the town of Chesapeake, near Portsmouth, in 1586. During the Revolution both Benedict Arnold and Cornwallis were in Portsmouth.

Norfolk Navy Yard (Open to Visitors During Exposition from 9 a. m. to 5 p. m. Except Sunday).

Both cities lay claim to this important government industry. Electric cars stop in front of the Portsmouth Ferry, and connect with the Yards. At the entrance, the visitor is instructed to repair to the office, where a pass will be issued to enter the grounds. Nearly 3,000 men are employed here, and the annual pay roll amounts to $2,500,000. The Yards have cost the government more than $20,000,000, and the annual repairs and improvements amount to $3,000,000. A dry-dock is under course of construction and with the marine barracks when completed, will make this station the greatest on the Atlantic coast. Here are located mammoth machine-shops and woodworking establishments where the interior fittings of ships are constructed. Men-of-war are sent to these yards for overhauling and general repairs.

On the opposite side of the Elizabeth River is the Training Station, which, with the exception of the one at Newport, R. I., is the largest in the United States. Here apprentice seamen receive their training, four months being the limit for recruits. The old men-of-war, Franklin and Richmond, have been fitted up as receiving-ships and three converted yachts, the Siren, Hornet and Restler, and a sailing yacht, the Eagle, are used for giving the recruits actual experience in handling a ship and in loading and manning guns.

An artificer's school is also attached to this branch of the service, where recruits receive a thorough mechanical training. On the Franklin, a bandsmen's school is held where enlisted musicians are trained. A Reserve Flotilla station is maintained south of the Training Station. The torpedo-boat crews are quartered aboard the U. S. ship Atlanta.

Tourists are sometimes allowed to visit men-of-war, at certain hours on special days allotted for that purpose.

Here at these yards seven ships have been built for the navy, the battleship Texas and the cruiser Raleigh being the two latest ones. The staunch old Constellation was built and launched here; also the Alliance, the Richmond and the Jamestown.

More than thirty large buildings are included in the yards. There are three dry-docks and one wet-dock large enough for several ships. The oldest one is built of stone and was begun Dec. 1, 1827. An interesting sight is an enormous pile of anchors dating back to the beginning of the navy. The yard contains 359 1-10 acres in Portsmouth and 91 acres in Norfolk. It was given the name "Norfolk Navy Yard" to distinguish it from the one at Portsmouth, N. H.

Trophy Park.—The first object that attracts the visitor upon entering the yards is the Park, which separates the offices from the workshops and wharves.

Here may be seen naval guns of many nations, types and ages. Spanish guns from men-of-war belonging to Admiral Cervera's fleet; relics and trophies from the Revolutionary War, the War of 1812, and from the Mexican, Civil and Spanish-American Wars, including guns captured at Tien-Tsin during the Boxer troubles, in 1900.

Specimens of armor from the Confederate ram Texas and the Albemarle are grouped about the flag-staff in the center of the Park. The torpedo tubes with two torpedoes captured with the Reina Mercedes can be seen at one end of the Park, while nearby are two guns from the famous U. S. ship Huron, wrecked off the North Carolina coast.

The large cannon-ball made entirely of stone, brought from Constantinople, is also most interesting. It represents the first cannon-balls ever used and it would fill the muzzle of the largest gun now in existence. Four carronades bearing the words, "Republica de Yucatan" were captured in the war with Mexico. Four larger ones were taken on the lakes from the British during the War of 1812.

In 1861 the Federal troops evacuated the yards and the U. S. battleship Pennsylvania was burned to the water's edge.

Naval Hospital.—About one mile from the Navy Yard. The grounds surrounding the hospital cover seventy-five acres. Admiral Cervera was held here on parole as a prisoner of war. A monument on the grounds marks the site of old Fort Nelson of Revolutionary fame.

The granite hospital building was erected 1835-6. The grounds were acquired by the Navy Department in 1827. The building has been used for hospital purposes during every American war that has occurred since its erection. A cemetery is attached to the

TRINITY CHURCH, PORTSMOUTH

grounds where a number of prominent men are buried. Nearly sixty Confederate soldiers and sailors are also interred in these grounds. A monument erected to the memory of soldiers and sailors buried here was unveiled by President Roosevelt, Memorial Day, May 30, 1906.

Trinity Church (High and Court Street).—This beautiful edifice was erected 1762; rebuilt 1829 and remodeled in 1893. During the Civil War the building was occupied by Federal troops as a hospital and during the War of 1812 it was converted into barracks.

The original roof still remains, blackened with age. In the old churchyard are many tombs with quaint inscriptions reminding one of the vicissitudes of time and war. Here lies buried Commodore Barron, who during the War of 1812 was suspended from the service and later restored, subsequently (1820) killing Commodore Decatur in a duel.

Confederate Monument (at the intersection of High and Court Streets, opposite Trinity Church).—At the base of the shaft on each corner is a life size figure of a Confederate soldier, each one representing a different division of the service. A tablet upon the monument reads:

> "In memory of Maj. F. W. Jett, C. Sa., to whose labor and devotion the erection of this monument is principally due."

Quaint old Portsmouth, with its historic associations, is still an important factor in the life of the government and its work shops, its navy yard, hospital, training schools and its old historic church possess a charm that will attract visitors for years to come.

CHAPTER V.

Newport News has a population of some 30,000 people. It was early known as "New Pork Neuces." Locally, Newport is pronounced "New'put."

It was near this point that the despondent Jamestown settlers first caught sight of Lord Delaware's

DRY DOCKS, NEWPORT NEWS

ships of relief in 1610. The arrival of this timely aid gave the colonists new courage and they turned back to their abandoned homes, thus saving the colony and insuring its future; a future so pregnant with significant events.

The Chesapeake and Ohio Railway has its terminus here and seventeen steamship lines connect with this city. Newport News is on Hampton Roads, where hundreds of ships coal. As much as 350,000 tons of coal arrive here in a month. Electric lines connect with Hampton, Old Point and Fortress Monroe and boats reach Norfolk in fifty minutes, Exposition grounds in twenty minutes, Jamestown Island and Yorktown in a few hours. Among other important industries located here are iron and brass foundries, shirt and shoe factories, planing mills, breweries and ice plants.

Ship Yards.—The chief point of interest, however, is the greatest ship building yards in America and the greatest dry-dock in the world. The plant cost over $15,000,000, and although a private concern, some of the largest American battleships have been built here; in fact, almost any day of the year ships in all stages of construction can be seen. Cruisers, battleships, submarines and torpedo boats are constantly being turned out. Seven thousand five hundred men are employed, and the weekly pay roll amounts to $60,000. The largest derrick in the world is also located here. It easily handles 300,000 pounds at one time.

Half a day can be devoted to Newport News if time is pressing, and electric car can be taken from this point for Hampton.

CHAPTER VI.

HAMPTON, THE OLDEST CONTINUOUS SETTLEMENT IN THE UNITED STATES.

When the English first visited Virginia, Hampton was an Indian village, called Kecoughtan. The city is on the waters of Hampton Roads, nearly opposite the Exposition site. It is claimed to be the oldest continuous English settlement in America.

Driven by a gale into the Chesapeake, the original expedition with Capt. John Smith landed at Cape

SOLDIERS' HOME, HAMPTON

Henry, but being attacked by the savages, they sailed up Hampton Roads and anchored off Old Point, May 10, 1607, remaining in the vicinity of Hampton for several days before proceeding up the James. Settlement was effected by Lord De La Warr, July, 1610. He was re-enforced in May, 1611, by Sir Thomas Dale.

In 1616, John Rolfe wrote that the town had twenty inhabitants. In 1619, the House of Burgesses were petitioned to change the heathen name of Kecoughtan to one more befitting a community of Christians, so Elizabeth City was substituted, but no act of legis-

lation can entirely obliterate the imprint of these
early savages from our boundaries.

> "Their name is on your waters,
>   Ye may not wash it out.
> Their memory lieth on your hills,
>   Their baptism on your shore.
> Your everlasting rivers speak
>   Their dialect of yore."

In 1623, there lived within the parish John Layden
and his wife, Anna, the first English couple married in
Virginia. One of their three daughters, Virginia, was
the first English child born in America, after Virginia
Dare, of Roanoke Colony. The present town of Hampton was founded in 1680 by an act of the Legislature.

The tourist visiting Virginia for the first time is
early impressed with the number of historic churches,
nearly all of them surrounded by the sacred God's
Acre. As little by little the dauntless colonists penetrated the wilderness, the first permanent public building to be erected was always a church. In fact, every
ten miles a place of worship was established. Many
of these edifices have long since been destroyed and
forgotten, but a number of them have remained
through the centuries of war and famine, standing today, in beauty of architecture, the equal of their
English prototypes. One of the most interesting and
perhaps the most picturesque of these early colonial
churches is the one at Hampton.

St. John's Church (Queen's Street).—This parish
was named after Princess Elizabeth, daughter of King
James I, 1620. The first rector was the Rev. William
Mease. Not a trace of the first church remains, except
a few trees on the land now belonging to the Tabb
family, north of the road leading to Old Point, which
was once part of the glebe lands of the church. In
1716 one writer says the town had about one hundred

inhabitants, but no church; services being held in the Court House.

What is known as the second church existed at that time at Pembroke Farm, a mile west of Hampton. It was built about 1667. The site with adjoining land, consisting of nine acres, still belongs to the parish. Here are the tombs of some of the oldest inhabitants, many of the stones being of black marble. Among them is one erected in 1697 to the memory of Admiral Neville. It is the intention to use the old graveyard as a cemetery for the parish, after St. John's Church-yard becomes no longer available.

The present church building is the third one built in the parish. Erected 1728 and built of bricks made by Henry Cary. It seems to have remained undamaged during the Revolutionary War, but June 24-27, 1813, the town and church was sacked by the British under Admiral Cockburn, the church being turned into bar-racks. It was subsequently repaired and renamed St. John's Church, 1827, and consecrated by Bishop R. C. Moore, Friday, Jan. 8, 1830.

Many of the churches in this vicinity were occu-pied by troops during the Civil War or suffered through fire or depredations and St. John's Church proved no exception. On the night of Aug. 7, 1861, Hampton and its venerable old church were destroyed by fire. In proof of their loyalty, the inhabitants un-der Gen. Magruder set fire to their own homes to pre-vent them from falling into the hands of the Federal troops, and in the general conflagration that followed old St. John's took fire also. The original walls stood, however, and the structure was again restored, 1868-70. A tablet upon the church gives a short history of the edifice, followed by this quotation from Psalms:

"O, give thanks unto the Lord, for he is good; for his mercy endureth forever." Rev. C. Braxton Bryan, Rector, January, 1904."

In 1903 the Association for the Preservation of Virginia Antiquities, presented to the church a beautiful memorial stained glass window in honor of the Colo-

ST. JOHN'S CHURCH, HAMPTON

nial clergy of Elizabeth City parish. One of these early (1610-1620) ministers, Rev. Wm. Mease, is said to have served the original Jamestown Church after the death of "Good Maister Hunt."

Communion Service.—The church has in its possession a communion service made in London in 1618 and presented by Mary Robinson to a church at South Hampton Hundred. When this edifice was destroyed in 1622, Gov. Yeardly took the service to Jamestown and it was later given to Elizabeth City Parish, where it has since been in constant use.

Churchyard.—The graveyard of St. John's is exceptionally beautiful and the inscriptions on the tombs attract the attention of all visitors to this picturesque little city. At one side of the church is a neat, dignified statue in memory of the Confederate dead.

Hampton Normal and Agricultural Institute for negroes was established 1868 and is one of the most

CLASS IN DAIRYING.

important colleges for the colored race in America. Rev. Hollis B. Frissell, D. D., LL. D., is the principal. The object of the school is to prepare academic, mechanical and agricultural teachers for the Negro and Indian races. Over one hundred and twenty officers and teachers are employed and the attendance exceeds 1,200; 1,310 graduates have been sent out from the school and over 5,000 under-graduates.

The first cargo of negro slaves was landed not far from Hampton in 1619, a significant fact, when it is considered that this is the first institution founded for the industrial training of their emancipated descendants. Over 35 per cent of the graduates are either farmers or mechanics, and the Institute points with pride to the fact that Booker T. Washington's name is among the list of her alumni.

In 1878, Indians were also admitted, 120 of whom

CLASS IN WEAVING.

are now in attendance. The U. S. Government annually pays $167 for the board and clothing of each of these Indian pupils. The state contributes $10,-000 annually to the support of the school for agricultural and military training and $1,500,000 has already been secured as an endowment fund. There are 60 buildings, including shops, where eighteen trades are taught. The farm consists of 800 acres.

Symms-Eaton Free School.—The oldest free school in America being founded in 1634 in memory of Benj. Symms and Thos. Eaton, who endowed it. This school, located at Hampton, is now a part of the regular public school system.

CHAPTER VII.

Having been driven from Cape Henry by the savages in 1607, the original explorers who later settled at Jamestown, weighed anchor in the shelter of this harbor, which, in thankfulness for protection from the storm at sea, they named "Point Comfort."

Palatial steamers touch at the Point on their way from Cape Charles to Norfolk and from northern ports, for Old Point is a resort whose fame is world wide. Thousands of tourists are entertained annually at the Hotel Chamberlain, which has been the scene of many a noted diplomatic and social function. Located directly on the waters of Hampton Roads, the glimmering lights of the Exposition are discernible directly opposite.

Fortress Monroe.—History records that as early as 1611 there was a fort at Point Comfort called "Fort Algernon." It was garrisoned by forty men, and contained seven iron cannons. In 1630, according to one historian, a larger and more pretentious fort was built. These fortifications were augmented from time to time, and in 1813 the garrison numbered 450 men, who made a gallant defense against the invasion of the British under Admiral Cockburn. Outnumbered, however, the Americans were forced to retreat.

The present fortifications, commenced in 1817 and completed in 1875, embrace a parapet wall a mile and a quarter long, enclosing eighty-six acres, and costing $2,258,453.05. The fortress is partially washed by the waters of Hampton Roads, and separated from the mainland by a wide and deep moat. All the latest disappearing guns, and modern machinery of war are here in evidence. During the Civil War the garrison aided the Federal men-of-war, the battery at the Rip Raps responding, in the famous battle of the Monitor and Merrimac.

The fortress, one of the best equipped in America, is the chief artillery station of the United States government, and is in reality a practical school for the

Copyright, 1906, by Cheyne Studio
MOAT, FORTRESS MONROE

army and navy. It has the longest line of fortifications in the world, and is ranked next to Gibraltar in importance.

Oct. 31, 1828, Edgar Allan Poe, who had enlisted in the army as Edgar A. Perry, was transferred from Battery H. of the First Artillery at Fort Moultrie, South Carolina, to Fortress Monroe. He was made company clerk and assistant in the commissariat department, and later promoted to the rank of sergeant major. April 15, 1829, he was honorably discharged with the highest encomiums from the officers under whom he had served.

On the spacious parade grounds may be seen the morning and evening drills of the soldiers, and in the park, and along the walks are many interesting guns, cannon-balls and other relics from the wars of the past. It was here that Jefferson Davis, the President of the Confederacy, was confined at the close of the Civil War, and it was this fortress the Spaniards planned to attack during the Spanish-American War. Its grim old walls have witnessed history in the making, and the waters surrounding it have rocked the very ''Cradle of the Republic.''

Rip Raps.—(Fort Wool, before the Civil War called Ft. Calhoun.) This is a fine granite fort, with earthworks within and without, situated between Fortress Monroe and the Exposition grounds. It is built upon an artificial island, and cost the government $16,000,-000. It commands the entrance to Chesapeake Bay, and is equipped with immense disappearing guns and the latest machinery for defense in time of war. With Fortress Monroe and the Rip Raps, tidewater Virginia is amply protected from the assault of any possible enemy by water.

CHAPTER VIII.

The Far East has its Mecca, Palestine its Jerusalem, France its Lourdes and Italy its Loretto, but America's only shrines are her altars of patriotism—the first and the most potent being Jamestown; Jamestown, the sire of Virginia, and Virginia the mother of this great Republic.

The site of old "James Towne" was originally a peninsula jutting into the James River, some forty miles from its mouth. Time, however, has cut the narrow neck of land connecting it with the mainland, leaving it stranded and isolated, the prey of the winds and the waves, which have slowly been obliterating its shores. An early colonial secretary records that the site was originally about two and three-quarters miles in length, and about one and one-quarter miles in width, and in some places only 300 yards wide. The peninsula crossed what is now known as Sandy Bay.

The place where the brave explorers landed, now over four hundred and fifty feet from the shore, lies buried under the waters of the James River. It is estimated to be about 1,500 feet west of the present wharf.

The government has just completed a permanent sea-wall around the entire island to protect it from the ravages of the river. It has been estimated that about twenty acres have been washed away. Twenty-three acres, where most of the original town was built, has been deeded to the Association for the Preservation of Virginia Antiquities by its former owners, Mr. and Mrs. Edw. E. Barney. The Association has endeavored to protect the old ruins, and the historic ivy-mantled tower from further devastation, and many excavations have been made under its auspices.

A concise description and history of the settlement at Jamestown has been given in one of the preliminary chapters. As the Exposition was inaugurated as the

CHURCH TOWER RUINS, JAMESTOWN

third centennial of that event, this history has been introduced at the beginning of this narrative, but before visiting the Island, the tourist should again read it over carefully.

The Jamestown Church.—History records that the first church, ''a homely thing, like a barn, set upon crotchets, covered with rafts, sedge and earth,'' was burned, with the settlement, about eight months after its erection.

A second church, within the entrenchments still in evidence, was built in time for the arrival of Lord Delaware in 1610. The communion table was of black walnut, the chancel, pulpit and pews of cedar and the "front hewn hollow like a canoe."

The day of Delaware's arrival, attended by a red-coated guard, he repaired to this church, delivered an address at the close of the sermon by Rev. Richard Buck. The third church was completed 1619 on the site of the present tower ruins. This edifice was evidently of frame construction. Its foundations have recently been unearthed within the boundaries of the brick church.

The Rev. Richard Buck also preached in the third church, and it was here that Gov. Yeardly called together the first Legislative Assembly in the New World.

The fourth church, represented by the present tower ruins, was completed between 1639 and 1644. It was built of blue and red glazed bricks, by some claimed to have been manufactured in the colony, and by others said to have been imported from England. The tower is believed to have been erected as much for defense against the Indians as for church purposes.

The original communion service, consisting of three pieces, presented in 1661 by the acting Governor, is now in possession of the Bruton Church at Williamsburg. Each piece bears the inscription:

"Mixe not holy things with profane. Ex dono francisci Morrison, Armiger, Anno Domi, 1661."

In 1676, during the turbulent days of Bacon's Rebellion, the church belonging to the present tower was destroyed with the town by fire. After the rebellion,

the church was again rebuilt, but about the end of the
seventeenth century it was deserted. It is the intention of the Colonial Dames of America to erect a
memorial church over the site of the old walls, which
recently have been unearthed. The Colonial Bell Association intends to hang a bell in the old tower, and
the Episcopal Church of America will place a tablet
within the church in honor of the first minister to
Jamestown, the Rev. Robert Hunt.

PARSON BLAIR'S TOMB, JAMESTOWN

The Graveyard.—Immediately surrounding the old
church is the graveyard, which undoubtedly was the
original burying ground of the colonists. The wall
marking its boundaries was built early in the eighteenth century. Beneath the nave and chancel of the
church, many important colonists were laid to rest.

An ironstone tablet bearing an impression of a coat-of-arms can still be seen, as well as the tombstone of Rev. John Clough, incumbent during Bacon's Rebellion, who died January, 1683. Among other inscriptions upon the gravestones in the churchyard we read:

"Here lies William Sherwood, that was born in the Parish of White Chappell, near London, a great sinner waiting for a Joyfull Resurrection."

One of the most interesting tombs is that of Parson Blair, minister at Jamestown, founder and first president of William and Mary College, and rector of Bruton Church at Williamsburg. He was also a member of the Council and Commissary to the Bishop of London. A long Latin inscription records the good doctor's accomplishments. An old sycamore tree has grown up between his grave and that of his wife, Sarah, shattering both tombstones.

Lady Frances Berkeley, wife of the colonial governor of that name, and Mrs. Edward Ambler, who as Mary Cary was courted by George Washington, are also buried here, in the northeast corner of the yard.

State House Ruins.—The third and fourth state houses, built on the same site, evidently faced the south, with a square porch in front. It was before the state house built in 1666 (the third one) that Nathaniel Bacon brought his determined followers to demand of Governor Berkeley a commission to raise troops to protect the settlers from Indian massacres. Thinking Bacon had merely come to revenge himself for the repeated insults heaped upon him, the choleric governor rushed out to meet him, and baring his breast, dramatically cried: "Here, shoot me, 'fore God, fair mark, shoot!"

"Sir," replied Bacon, "my sword shall rust in its scabbard before even a hair of your head is touched."

The following year, the building was burned by Bacon's men and until the fourth State House was built, in 1686, the Council were compelled to meet in the taverns of the town. The last House was also destroyed by fire in 1698, and the next year the capital was removed to Williamsburg. The foundations of these two buildings still remain, mute witnesses to the struggles of our early legislators in the arena of colonial politics.

Ambler Ruin.—East of the tower are the ruins of the Jacqueline Ambler Mansion. It was burned during the Civil War, rebuilt and again destroyed by fire in 1896. This was the home of Washington's sweetheart, Mary Cary.

Ludwell Houses.—Three ruins next to the State House mark the site of houses owned by Philip Ludwell, Governor of North Carolina, and third husband of Governor Berkeley's widow. In the cellar of the one at the end of the row, the "Country House," were found a pipe, scissors, copper candlestick, two bombshells and other curious articles, which have been safeguarded under the Tower by the Association for the Preservation of Virginia Antiquities.

Other Landmarks.—East of the tower was located the later acquisitions to Jamestown, called "New Towne," supposed to have been built during the administration of Governor George Yardley, who entered upon his duties in 1619.

Traces of a foundation have been found less than two hundred feet from the wharf, which may have been that of the first State House, built 1630. Other foundations can be seen along the river bank. The site of the second fort, known as Turf Fort, has been located, but no trace of its foundations remains. Embankments and fortifications of the Confederates are clearly in evidence. At the east end of the island is the Travis private burial ground only two of the stones remaining legible.

From Jamestown one can proceed overland to the most famous village in the United States—Williamsburg, seven miles distant. A macadam road has been built between the island and Williamsburg, and the

RUINS COLONIAL GOVERNOR'S MANSION

trip can be made by automobile or by stage, with much pleasure and profit.

It is with a deep feeling of reverence that one turns his back upon these sacred ruins, gaunt and bare, denuded by three centuries of cankering storms, all that is left to mark the feverish lives of the Nation's founders, many of whom sleep in long forgotten graves.

MAP OF

OLD-HISTORIC WILLIAMSBURG.

A. William and Mary College.
B. Brafferton.
C. President's House.
D. Blair House.
E. Bruton Church.

F. Wythe House.
G. Governor's Palace Site.
H. Audrey House.
I. Court House.
J. Powder Horn.
K. Baptist Church.
L. Ancient Masonic Temple.

M. Site House of Burgesses.
N. Site first Theater in U. S.
O. Peyton Randolph House.
P. Tazewell Hall.
Q. Martha Washington Kitchen.
R. Hospital.
S. Debtors' Prison.
T. Bassett Hall.
U. Cary House.
V. Old Home of Blackbeard, the Pirate
W. Colonial Inn.
X. Site Old Raleigh Tavern.

CHAPTER IX

Although the birth of the Nation took place at Jamestown, it was at Williamsburg that the infant government was prepared to assume her position as a full fledged Republic.

The annals of this little village, unbroken for over two centuries, are pregnant with momentous records of past achievements. More historic associations cluster around this quiet hamlet than any other existing American town or city. Here more significant events have taken place than are recorded in the chronicles of any other borough. Its streets are fairly haunted by the personalities of the great; echoing and re-echoing with the names of titled governors, eloquent orators, brilliant statesmen, astute theologians and brave warriors of world-wide reputation.

Here, in stately magnificence, ruled the representatives of the British Crown: Spotswood, Drysdale, Gooch, Dinwiddie, Fauquier, Botetourt and Dunmore. Before the Colonial House of Burgesses appeared Washington, Patrick Henry and other eminent men. Here lived Sir John Randolph, Edmund and Peyton Randolph and John Blair and from historic old William and Mary College graduated a host of famous men, whose names have been recorded upon the scrolls of the nation, among them Jefferson, Monroe, Tyler and Chief Justice Marshall.

Suddenly transported from the bustling streets of a twentieth century city to the historic avenues of old Williamsburg, the visitor actually feels that time has turned back the calendar at least two centuries. Here are many of the original structures, standing intact as they did when occupied by our Colonial forefathers. The same old brass knockers which echoed under the impetus of many a famous hand still remain upon the same old doors that opened in hospitable welcome to bygone dignitaries, warriors and heroes. Even the furnishings of many of the present homes consist of heirlooms handed down from one generation to another; original Chippendale tables and chairs, silver candle-sticks, brass andirons and countless other treasures that remind us of the grandeur of Colonial days. Even many of the citizens are direct descendants of the early pioneers, occupying the same houses, using the same furniture and displaying in their lives the same hospitable traits that characterized their ancestors.

Williamsburg, by all means, should be placed in the hands of the United States Government as a National Reservation. So far as possible, the old historic buildings that have been razed should be rebuilt. The Governor's Palace and the original House of Burgesses should be reconstructed. The Speaker's old chair and the stove, now at the Richmond Capitol, should be returned to Williamsburg. Historical documents, relics and Colonial furniture should be gathered and used in making these buildings replicas of those existing during the infancy of the nation. Public subscription would do much toward this end and Williamsburg would become the true Mecca for every patriotic American.

Teachers and pupils should be sent to visit these historic associations. Washington, Jefferson, Patrick

Henry are now merely names we conjure with, but no one can visit Old Bruton Church or stand upon the foundations of the Old House of Burgesses, without feeling the actual personality of these men as stamped upon the historic walls of Williamsburg. They would no longer remain mere names, but would become the embodiment of real characters who lived and fought and died for their country.

Williamsburg, originally known as Middle Plantation, was laid out by Gov. Sir John Harvey in 1632. In 1648 ''Harrop Parish,'' in James City, was united with Middle Plantation and called Middletown Parish and in 1674 Marston Parish, York County, was added and the name changed to Bruton Parish. The town was named in honor of the English sovereigns, William and Mary, and boasts of a royal charter. In 1699, after the desertion of Jamestown, the Capital was removed to Williamsburg and Bruton Church became the direct successor of the Court Church of Virginia.

The original plan provided for laying the town out in the form of a W and M, in honor of William and Mary, but it was abandoned as impracticable. The streets were platted by Gov. Francis Nicholson, in 1698, and named in honor of British associations: England, Scotland, Ireland, Duke of Gloucester, Prince, Duke, Queen, George, Henry, York and similar names.

With the idea of keeping church and state apart, the House of Burgesses was located at one end of the Duke of Gloucester street, and at the other extremity, nearly a mile distant, William and Mary College. Shaded by trees on both sides, with lamp-posts extending down the center, the Duke of Gloucester

Street, ninety feet wide, forms one of the most attractive village streets in America. This was the Colonial Boulevard and down this avenue in coach, berlin or chaise were often seen the titled gentry and aristocrats of Colonial Virginia, on their way to Bruton Church. This street was named in honor of William, Duke of Gloucester, eldest son of Queen Anne.

Many a novelist of national reputation has made historic old Williamsburg the scene of plot and story and visitors will renew many a familiar memory as they gaze upon these evidences of a past grandeur.

Bruton Church (Duke of Gloucester Street).—The Court Church of Colonial Virginia and the mother of the Episcopal Church in America. In all the broad domain of the United States, there is no one building surrounded by more historic associations than this venerable old church. Here worshipped George Washington, Thomas Jefferson, Madison, Monroe and Tyler; here sat the Colonial Governors and the members of the House of Burgesses; the Harrisons, Pendletons, Patrick Henry, the Randolphs, the Lees and many other illustrious dignitaries, and from this church emanated the religious, social and political life that characterized the Old Dominion.

Bruton Church, evidently named from Bruton, Somerset, England, the home of Gov. Berkeley, was founded in 1632. Prior to 1665 there was a small frame church of which little is known, but the second church, built of brick, was erected on land donated by Col. John Page, 1683. The present structure, designed by Gov. Alexander Spotswood, was built of blue and red glazed brick, in 1710.

Here worshipped the Colonial Governors and members of the House of Burgesses. A large square pew was provided for the governor and a beautiful silk drapery hung from brass supports, secluding him from the rest of the congregation when desired. The pews for the members of the House were placed together across the transepts. This part of the church

BRUTON CHURCH, WILLIAMSBURG

was built by and for the members of the House of Burgesses.

The old Register, badly mutilated, found a few years ago, contains records from 1662 to 1797. The first entry in the vestry book is dated April 18, 1674. November 29, 1683, the volume records: "The Parish Church is at length completed." The fees of the Parish clerk were "three pounds of tobacco for registering every christening and burial in ye Parish." The "Sexton to have ten of tobacco for every

grave that he diggs.'' June 5, 1682, it was agreed that
the rector be paid ''ye sum of sixteen thousand, six
hundred and sixty-six pounds of tobacco and caske.''

In 1699, the Jamestown Church was abandoned
with the town, and Bruton Church became its recog-
nized successor. The font, which tradition says is
the one from which Pocahontas was baptized, together with the Communion Service, was given into
the keeping of Bruton Church, where they still may
be seen. The Jamestown service consists of a chalice,
paten and alms basin, the two former presented by
Francis Morrison.

Two other services are in the possession of the
Church: The Bruton Parish Church Service, known
as the ''Queen Anne Set,'' consisting of Cup and
Cover, dated 1686, and Paten, dated 1737; also the
King George Service, consisting of Flagon, dated
1766, chalice, 1764, and alms basin, all bearing the
Royal Arms.

The bell in the tower was presented to the Parish
in 1761, by James Tarpley. Toward the close of the
seventeenth century the old church seemed to be in
need of constant repair and in 1706 twenty thousand
pounds of tobacco were levied toward a new structure—the present one, which was completed in 1715,
during the ministry of Rev. Mr. Blair.

The churchyard wall was completed in 1754 by
Samuel Spurr, for £320. The site for the church and
graveyard was the gift of John Page, Nov. 14, 1678,
the yard fronting on Duke of Gloucester Street, for
three hundred feet.

The Rev. W. A. R. Goodwin, A. M., present rector
of the church, has given a graphic description of the
service in Colonial Days in his ''Historical Sketches

of Bruton Church.'' which we take the liberty of quoting, in part:

''The old bell breaks the stillness of the Sabbath morn. Old fashioned coaches drive up to the gate, and as the door is opened by a liveried footman, the occupants come forth clothed after the last year's fashion of the Court of George the Third. Around the door the Colonial gentry are assembled. From Raleigh Tavern there comes a group of men who are representatives of the people in the House of Burgesses. The Governor's carriage sweeps down the Palace Green and draws up before the door.

''We pass into the church. In spite of all the care we take, our footsteps resound through the building as we walk down the flagstone aisle. Passing into a large square pew, we close the door and wait. It is difficult to see those in front of us. We notice that the men sit on the north side of the church, and the women on the south. Mr. Peter Pelham enters and ascending the 'Organ loft' begins to play the new organ, recently purchased in England for the church by order of the House of Burgesses. The students from the College of William and Mary enter, attended by one of the Masters, and file into the gallery assigned to them in the south wing of the church. When the students have all entered the gallery door is locked, and the key given to the sexton. There is no chance now for them to escape.

''By an outside stairway, leading up to the gallery in the north wing, we see the servants of the parishioners enter. The door at the west, leading from the tower, opens and the minister, who has vested there, enters and, passing down the aisle, enters the chancel at the east end of the church. The clerk takes his place at the desk below the pulpit, which stands down in the body of the building at the southeast corner of the church.

"And now, even over the high back pews, we can see that something is attracting general attention. The tower door opens, and the Court Procession enters, His Excellency, the Governor, passes down the aisle to his pew. It is in the chancel end of the church, on the north side of the aisle; it is elevated from the floor. A silk canopy hangs over it, and around it in large letters of gold is the Governor's name. The Counsel of state, and the members of the House of Burgesses, and the Surveyor-General take pews officially assigned. The service begins. The beadle keeps his eye upon the college youth in particular. We hear what sounds like an imprecation from a nearby pew when the prayer is said for George the Third, and the Royal Family, but it is discreetly suppressed.

"The service ended, the minister ascends the high steps leading up into the southeast corner pulpit, takes his text and begins his sermon. Those who have brought braziers with which to warm their feet listen with comfort, if not always with patience. The benediction said, groups gather in the church and exchange greetings, collect the news, discuss the sermon and exchange opinions, and go to their homes."[*]

The so-called "modern improvements" added to the church, commenced April 18, 1829, when it was resolved to cut down the pews. In 1839 the interior of the church was remodeled by building a partition across the interior, changing the shape from a cross to a T. The chancel was moved and built out from

[*]Bruton Parish Church, Restored, by Rev. W. A. R. Goodwin.

this partition, the old pulpit removed with the flag-stone aisle and the tower converted into a coal-bin.

During the Civil War no service was held in the edifice, because the authorities required that the prayer for the President of the United States be said, so it was used as a Confederate hospital.

In 1886, another innovation in the interior was installed, the gallery in the north end removed and other changes made. In 1903, at the suggestion of Rev. W. A. R. Goodwin, the rector, it was decided to restore the church to its original Colonial form. The architects, Messrs. Barney and Chapman, of New York, who donated their services, estimated the cost of restoration to be $27,000, $14,000 for structural repairs and $13,000 for restoration of the interior, and May 14, 1905, the work began.

In excavating, twenty-eight graves were found under the chancel and aisles, some of which were identified and marked by memorial slabs. These graves are indicated by numbers on the diagram shown on page 64.

Memorials are to be erected to ''some of the distinguished statesmen and Parish Vestrymen of the Colonial and Revolutionary period, who worshipped in the building, or resided there while representing the people of Virginia in the House of Burgesses, or the Sovereign Authority of England, as Governors or as Members of the Council.'' His Majesty, King Edward, has contributed a memorial Bible and His Excellency, Theodore Roosevelt, has given a lectern to hold it. Among other memorials will be a silver alms basin to Rev. Robert Hunt, the first minister at Jamestown.

Restoration of the clock formerly in the old

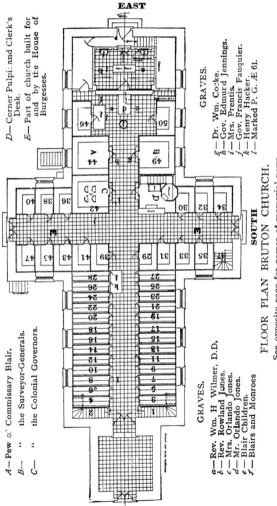

EAST

NORTH

SOUTH

WEST

D—Corner Pulpit and Clerk's Desk.

E—Part of church built for and by the House of Burgesses.

A—Pew of Commissary Blair.

B—   "   the Surveyor-Generals.

C—   "   the Colonial Governors.

GRAVES.

g—Dr. Wm. Cocke.

h—Gov. Edmund Jennings.

i—Mrs. Prentis.

j—Gov. Francis Fauquier.

k—Henry Hacker.

l—Marked P. G. Æ 61.

FLOOR PLAN BRUTON CHURCH.

See opposite page for names of memorial pews.

GRAVES.

a—Rev. Wm. H Wilmer, D.D.

b—Rev. Rowland Jones.

c—Mrs. Orlando Jones.

d—Mr. Orlando Jones.

e—Blair Children.

f—Blairs and Monroes

Williamsburg Capitol is to be made in honor of the House of Burgesses. Tablets to the Colonial Governors and Members of the Council, Secretaries of State, Receivers General, Auditors General, to the Colonial Clergy, to the later Rectors and to the Rev. Commissary, James Blair, D.D., are to be erected. The entrance gate to the churchyard is to be a memorial to General George Washington, who was a regular attendent at old Bruton. The pews have also been made memorials to other dignitaries as follows:

MEMORIAL PEWS IN BRUTON CHURCH.

Pew No. 1 (Nave)—Hon. Thomas Peale (1662 and 1684), and Col. Thomas Ballard (1670), Members of the Council and Vestrymen.

Pew No. 2—Colonial Church Wardens of the Parish (1674-1768).

Pew No. 3—Capt. Thos. Thorp (1693), Thomas Pettus (1698), Vestrymen.

Pew No. 4—Hon. Edward Barradall, Kt. (1735), Vestryman; Attorney General, 1737-1743.

Pew No. 5—Wm. Hansford (1704), Henry Cary (1721), Vestrymen.

Pew No. 6—Michael Archer (1721) and James Archer, Vestrymen.

Pew No. 7—James Bray, Vestryman (1674), and member of Council (1670), David Bray (1684), Thomas Bray and David Bray, Jr.

Pew No. 8—James Whaley (1701), Thomas Whaley (1769), Vestrymen.

Pew No. 9—William Parks, Vestryman and Editor of First Virginia Gazette (1736).

Pew No. 10—William Robertson, Clerk of the Council, (1705), Vestryman prior to 1768; Thomas Everard, Vestryman, 1769.

Pew No. 11—Samuel Timson, William Timson, Sr., Vestrymen (1702), William Timson, Jr.

Pew No. 12—John Prentis, Vestryman (1769); William Prentis, Vestryman; Joseph Prentis, M. H. B., 1775.

Pew No. 13—Capt. Hugh Norvell (1694), George Norvell and William Norvell, Vestrymen and M. H. B. (1775).

Pew No. 14—Hon. Thomas Ludwell, M. H. B., Vestryman, 1685.

Pew No. 15—Gideon Macon, M. H. B., 1696; Vestryman, 1678.

Pew No. 16—Hon. Edmund Jenings, M. H. B., Secretary of State, Vestryman, 1694.

Pew No. 17—Philip Ludwell, M. H. B., Auditor General (Vestryman 1684), 1688.

Pew No. 18—Benjamin Waller, M. H. B. (Vestryman), 1744, Judge of Court of Admiralty, 1744.

Pew No. 19 (Nave)—Memory of the Vestry of 1674-1683, who erected the first brick church upon this foundation.

Pew No. 20—Memory of the Vestry of 1710-1715, who erected the present church building, the Coöperating Committee of the House of Burgesses and the Contractor, James Morris.

Pew No. 21—Lewis Burwell, Nathaniel Burwell and Armistead Burwell (Vestrymen).

Pew No. 22 (Nave)—Attorneys General of Virginia, 1697 to 1776.

Pew No. 23 (Nave)—John Custis, Member of Council, Surveyor-General, Vestryman (1721), Daniel Parke Custis, Mrs. Martha Custis.

Pew No. 24 (Nave)—Edmund Randolph, Delegate to Congress, 1779-82; Governor of Virginia, 1786-8; Delegate Constitutional Convention, 1787; Attorney General, 1789-94; Secretary State, 1794-5.

Pew No. 25 (Nave)—Chief Justice John Marshall.

Pew No. 26 (Nave)—Sir John Randolph, Speaker H. B., 1736; Vestryman, 1729.

Pew No. 27 (Nave)—James Monroe, President United States.

Pew No. 28 (Nave)—John Tyler, 1837, President United States.

Pew No. 29 (Transept)—George Washington, President United States, Signer of Declaration of Independence.

Pew No. 30 (Transept)—Patrick Henry, M. H. B.

Pew No. 31 (Transept)—Peyton Randolph, Vestryman, 1747; Attorney General, 1747-66; Speaker H. B., 1766-1775; President First Continental Congress, 1774, and Delegate to Congress, 1775.

Pew No. 32 (Transept)—George Mason, drafted Virginia Bill of Rights and Constitution, 1776.

Pew No. 33 (Transept)—Richard Bland.

Pew No. 34 (Transept)—Archibald Cary and Dabney Carr.

Pew No. 35 (Transept)—Robert Carter Nicholas, Vestryman, and Paul Carrington.

Pew No. 36 (Transept)—Edmund Pendleton, M. H. B., member Continental Congress, author resolutions submitted Virginia delegates asking for Declaration of Independence.

Pew No. 37 (Transept)—Memorial to the Speakers of the House of Burgesses, 1700 to 1775.

Pew No. 38 (Transept)—Dudley Digges and Andrew Lewis.

Pew No. 39 (Transept)—Thomas Jefferson, President United States, Signer of Declaration of Independence.

Pew No. 40 (Transept)—William Cabell and Joseph Cabell.

Pew No. 41 (Transept)—George Wythe, Vestryman and Signer of Declaration of Independence.

Pew No. 42 (Transept)—Memorial to the Colonial Governors and Members of the Council, 1698 to 1775.

Pew No. 43 (Transept)—Thomas Nelson, Secretary of State and Signer of Declaration of Independence.

Pew No. 44 (Choir)—Rev. Commissary James Blair, D. D., 1656-1743 ; Rector, 1710-1743 ; Dr. Archibald Blair ; John Blair, Auditor General (1), 1689-1771 ; Vestryman, 1744 ; John Blair, Judge United States Supreme Court (2).

Pew No. 45 (Transept)—Carter Braxton and Benjamin Harrison, Signers of Declaration of Independence.

Pew No. 46 (Choir)—Presidents of the College of William and Mary, 1693 to 1854.

Pew No. 47 (Transept)—Richard Henry Lee and Francis Lightfoot Lee, Signers of Declaration of Independence.

Pew No. 49 (Choir)—Surveyors General who occupied this pew, 1692 to 1728.

Pew No. 50 (Choir)—Col. John Page, Esq., 1627-1691-2 ; Vestryman, 1674.

The restoration of Old Bruton is largely due to the indefatigable efforts of Dr. Goodwin, the present rector, and his faithful corps of assistants, who have interested patriotic Americans from all parts of the United States in this noble work, which has practically been completed. A fireproof vault and steel safe have been provided for the preservation of the Communion Services and Vestry Records.

The old gallery where the students from the College were locked in has been retained, and upon the hacked railing can still be deciphered the names of Patrick Henry and other notable men, who, as boys, amused themselves during service by carving their names upon this railing with their jack-knives. The high backed pews, the Colonial Governor's and Surveyor General's pews, as well as those of the House of Burgesses, have been replaced together with the ancient old pupil and its sounding board.

As the rector has beautifully written: ''Old Bruton Church has well withstood the devastating touch of time. The storms of many winters have gone over it, the fierce battles of two great wars have raged near it, and in it have lain the sick and wounded of two armies, and yet it stands today, just as it stood well nigh two hundred years ago.''

> "The tramp of many a busy foot
>   Which sought thy aisles is o'er,
> And many a weary heart around
>   Is still'd forever more."

The Bruton Churchyard.—''The ivy clings to the mouldering wall and with each gust the dead leaves fall.''

As stated, the brick wall around the graveyard was built in 1754. Among the honeysuckle and magnolias, sleep many a forgotten hero, and the descendants of many a noted personage.

Near the north door of the church are buried the Curtis children, George Washington's step-children. Here are the tombs of Richard Kempe, Secretary of the Colony and member of the Council at Jamestown in 1642; also officiating Governor during Berkeley's absence. It was he who ordered ''that the eighteenth day of April be yearly celebrated by thanksgivings for our deliverance from the hands of the Savages,'' the first Thanksgiving Day in the Colony.

A queer epitaph is that upon the tombstone of Rev. Servant Jones:

> "Like the most of imperfect humanity, he was not exempt from some of its frailties, but a kinder soul seldom existed. He possessed in his nature a Bank of Benevolence, which secretly dispensed its varied blessings to the needy."

> "Time was when his cheek with life's crimson was flushed,
>   When cheerful his voice was, health sat on his brow;
> That cheek is now palsied, that voice is now hushed,
>   He sleeps with the dust of his first partner now."

He it was who said the following grace at a dinner given by one of his parishioners:

> "Good Lord of love look down from above,
>   And bless the owl who ate this fowl
> And left these bones for Scervant Jones."

He was a man of quaint ways and strange speech. He composed a touching tribute to his first wife, and ordered it engraved upon a tombstone. It is said that he brought the stone to Williamsburg upon the top of the coach in which he returned from his bridal trip with his second wife.

The epitaph reads:

"If woman ever yet did well,
If woman ever did excell,
If woman husband ere adored,
If woman ever loved the Lord.

If ever faith and hope and love
In human flesh did live and move,
If all the graces ere did meet
In her, in her they were complete.

My Ann, my all, my angel wife,
My dearest one, my love, my life,
I cannot sigh or say farewell.
But where thou dwellest I will dwell."

William and Mary College.—Situated at the extreme end of Duke of Gloucester Street, nearly a mile opposite from site of the House of Burgesses. The College was founded in 1693 through the efforts of its first President, Rev. James Blair, D.D., who was also rector of the Jamestown Church and later of Old Bruton. His tomb can still be seen at Jamestown, separated from that of his wife by a large sycamore.

The college designed by the famous architect, Sir Christopher Wren, also designer of St. Paul's Cathedral, London, was named in honor of the reigning sovereigns and with the exception of King's College (Columbia), is the only one in the United States that can boast of a royal charter. It is far from being a handsome structure and Jefferson called it "a rude, misshapen pile." The college colors are orange and white, in honor of the House of Orange. The original endowment was 1,985 pounds, 14 shillings and 10 pence and a penny per pound on all tobacco exported from Virginia. A queer condition of the charter reads that the authorities pay to "us and to

our successors, two copies of Latin verse yearly on the
fifth day of November, at the House of the Governor
or Lieutenant-Governor for the time being.''

For four years following the removal of the Capital
from Jamestown, the House of Burgesses met here.
George Washington is numbered among the chancel-
lors, also President Tyler, likewise a student. Other
notable students were Thomas Jefferson, James Monroe, Edmund and Peyton Randolph, Gen. Winfield
Scott and many others. The building was used as a
hospital during two wars and was burned in 1705,
1859 and again in 1863, but re-erected on the same
walls.

The first Greek letter society in the United States
was established here in 1776. The literary and art
treasures in the custody of the college are of in-
estimable value, many of them being gifts from
Colonial Governors and Presidents of the United
States. Under the Chapel are buried Lord Botetourt,
Governor from 1768-1770, Sir John Randolph, John
and Peyton Randolph and other notables.

Brafferton.—The first permanent Indian school in
the United States, established from funds derived
from the estate of Hon. Robert Boyle in 1691, was
built in 1723. It stands across from the President's
house, to the left of the main building, and is now
used for dormitories.

President's House.—Opposite Brafferton. Built in
1732 and accidentally burned by the French, who
were on their way to Yorktown. It was rebuilt at
the expense of Louis XVI. Prior to the siege of
Yorktown, Cornwallis used it for his headquarters.

Statue Lord Botetourt.—Before the College Building
on the campus, stands a monument to the best loved

of all the Colonial Governors, "The Right Honorable Norborne Berkeley, Baron de Botetourt." It was erected by the House of Burgesses in 1774. It was removed from its old location in the portico of the College in 1797.

The inscription on the right side of the monument reads as follows:

"Deeply impressed with the warmest sense of gratitude for his Excellency's, the Right Honorable Lord Botetourt's prudent and wise administration, and that the remembrance of those many public and social virtues, which so eminently adorned his illustrious character might be transmitted to posterity, the General Assembly of Virignia on the XX day of July, Ann. Dom MDCCLXXI, resolved with one united voice to erect this statue to his Lordship's memory. Let wisdom and justice preside in any country, the people must and will be happy." On the opposite side, the inscription reads:

"America, behold your friend, who, leaving his native country, declined those additional honors, which were there in store for him, that he might heal your wounds and restore tranquility and happiness to this extensive continent. With what zeal and anxiety he pursued these glorious objects, Virginia thus bears her grateful testimony."

House of Burgesses Site.—Directly opposite William and Mary College, at the extreme end of Duke of Gloucester Street, stood the stately House of Burgesses, the Capitol of the Old Dominion.

Nothing but the foundation walls remain to indicate the spot hallowed by so many historical associations, except a stone monument erected May 26, 1904, by the Association for the Preservation of Vir-

ginia Antiquities, in memory of the members of the
House of Burgesses. It was built in 1705, at the
expense of Queen Anne, but was burned in 1746 and
again in 1832. The original speaker's chair and the
stove used here are to be seen in the State Capitol
at Richmond.

It was here that Washington appeared to deliver
his historic message from St. Pierre to the House of
Burgesses, prior to the French and Indian War. It
was here that the Committee of Correspondence was
born under the guardianship of Dabney Carr. Here
the Committee of Safety was organized and here was
passed the celebrated Virginia Bill of Rights, which
more than any other action of the Colonists led directly to the Declaration of Independence.

On arrival of the odious Stamp Act, the House was
in session. One of the Burgesses, a young lawyer,
who as yet was noted only for his eloquence, offered
the first opposition to the Act in the Colonies, but
when that speech was finished, the name of Patrick
Henry electrified the Colonies, from Massachusetts to
Virginia, with startling fear and doubt. For the first
time in the history of the new world, the King was
publicly arraigned.

The King, said Patrick Henry, in assenting to the
taxing of the colonies, had acted the part of a
tyrant. Alluding to the fate of other tyrants, amid
the breathless suspense of his auditors, he continued:
''Caesar had his Brutus, Charles I his Cromwell, and
George III——''

A cry interrupted the speaker and broke the
nervous strain of the House. ''Treason!'' The word
echoed through the room, with the suddenness of a
thunderbolt, and then after a significant pause, the

white drawn, tense face of the young orator stood
out like a silhouette in the dimly lighted chamber, and
with uplifted arm, he leaned forward and defiantly
cried: "And George III may profit by their example.
If this be treason, make the most of it!"

In 1780 the Capital was removed from Williamsburg to Richmond, and in 1832 fire again destroyed
this historic old pile which witnessed so many thrill-
ing scenes in the early history of the nation. What

SITE OF THE HOUSE OF BURGESSES.

could be more fitting than the restoration of this first
Capitol of the infant Republic as a permanent museum
museum for Colonial relics.

The Palace Green and Governor's Palace.—Between
Bruton Church and the old Court House, is a long
strip of lawn known as the Palace Green. Originally,
each side of the Green consisted of a walk leading to

the Palace, shaded by beautiful lindens brought from Scotland. The grounds, including the Green, consisted of three hundred and seventy acres.

The Palace itself was situated at the end of the Green. Fifteen thousand dollars was appropriated by the Assembly for its erection. It is described by an early writer as "a magnificent structure, finished and beautified with gates, fine gardens, offices, walks, a fine canal, orchards, etc.

A peculiar feature of Colonial life were the "offices." In those days business men had separate buildings erected, generally at the side of their residences, which were used exclusively for office purposes. A number of these queer buildings are still standing in Williamsburg.

Lord Dunmore was the last Colonial Governor to occupy the Palace, and eight years after, following the siege of Yorktown, it was accidentally burned by some of the French troops. Nothing now remains of it, but the site.

Dunmore's Cave.—From the Palace cellars, an underground passage connected with a cave, now marked by an enclosed mound of earth about 500 feet back of the Palace Green. It is said that the Governor, who was in much disrepute among the Colonists, prepared it as a means of escape from their possible wrath.

The Powder Horn.—In the order of historical importance, perhaps the next Colonial landmark to be considered is the antique Powder Horn, an octagonal-shaped building, across from the Court House. In 1714, by special act of the House of Burgesses, Governor Spotswood drew the plans for a powder magaizne, its walls to be 22 inches thick and the entire building to be surrounded by brick walls 10 to 12 feet high, parallel with its sides, distant 21 feet.

Shortly before the Revolutionary War, Governor Dunmore made himself very obnoxious to the Colonists, the crowning feature of his perfidy being the midnight theft of some twenty barrels of powder from this magazine. This ammunition he conveyed to his ship, the "Magdalen," in the James River, four miles distant. Confronted by a demand for an explanation, presented by order of the Council, Aldermen and Mayor, he replied, that "Hearing of an insurrection in a neighboring county, I have removed the powder from the magazine."

This action of the Governor almost precipitated hostilities, and only through Washington's and Pendleton's influence were a company of minutemen prevented from marching from Fredericksburg to Williamsburg. Dunmore finally paid the Colony three hundred and thirty pounds sterling for the powder, but when the citizens came to examine the magazine, several barrels of powder were found hidden under the floor, together with a spring gun, which injured one of the investigators. This last act aroused such a storm that he fled to his man-of-war, "Fowey," anchored at Yorktown.

For several years the Powder Horn was used as a Baptist Church, with Rev. Servant Jones in charge. Later it was converted into a dancing school. During the Civil War, the Confederates used it as an arsenal, after which the town sold it and it became a common stable, but was eventually purchased by the Association for the Preservation of Virginia Antiquities, who have fitted it up for a museum. The wall around the Magazine was torn down and the bricks used, in 1856, for the foundation of the Baptist Church.

Court House (Duke of Gloucester Street).—Built 1769. Its columnless porch and high belfry are especially noticeable features. This old building was the scene of many an important prerevolutionary debate. Its interior remains practically unchanged.

The center room is for the Court and in the rear of it is a raised platform for the judge. Immediately in front sat the jury in a semi-circle with their backs

COURT HOUSE, WILLIAMSBURG.

to the judge, so that neither judge nor jury could be influenced by each other's changing expressions. In an opposite semi-circle, facing the judge and jury, sat the lawyers, thus completing the circle. Behind the lawyers are three pew-like seats, one for the prisoner in the center, one for the sheriff on one side, and one for the witnesses on the other side.

Wythe House.—In the rear of Bruton Church, on Palace Street, facing the Green, is one of the most interesting Colonial houses in the village. This was the home of the man who devised the seal of Virginia—a member of the Virginia Convention for the ratification of the Constitution and a student and chancellor of William and Mary College—George Wythe, the patriot.

The house was used by Washington as headquarters prior to the siege of Yorktown, and it is said that on moonlight nights the ghost of the

WYTHE HOUSE, WASHINGTON'S HEADQUARTERS.

"Father of his Country" appears in the hall with clanking sword at his side. The bedroom of Judge Wythe is also said to be haunted, a cold white hand appearing and pressing the brow of anyone who occupies it. The ghost of Lady Skipwith, daughter of the master of Westover, is said to be seen, slowly descending the Colonial stairway, with slow and dignified step.

The flooring in this old house consists of boards that run the full length of the rooms without piece or patch, and the deep walls and window recesses show how well our forefathers built—better, perhaps, than they knew.

In the "Voice of the People," Ellen Glasgow has made it the home of one of her principal characters, "Judge Bassett." It is now occupied by a sweet-faced, grey-haired maiden lady, who finds her chief delight in showing the old mansion to the many patriotic pilgrims, who clamor for a glimpse of this famous haunted house.

Audrey's House.—Diagonally opposite from the Wythe House, on Dunmore Street, stands a modest little residence, called the "Audrey House," said to have been the home of Miss Mary Johnston's "Audrey," described in her novel of that name. The real romance connected with the house is the inscription, evidently scratched with a diamond ring, on one of the tiny window panes.

J B.

1796 Nov 23 O fatal day

What a volume of romance lies hidden in that "O, fatal day." The house is now occupied by Miss Estelle Smith, who has made a study of the historic associations which cluster around Williamsburg and Jamestown. She has carefully searched all records for any important happening on Nov. 23, 1796, but without avail, so it is reasonable to presume that the tragedy must have been one of the heart—a personal incident and not one of public significance.

Debtor's Prison.—One of the dark spots on the pages of our Colonial history is the sad record of imprisonment for debt, and here in Williamsburg is a building said to have been used for the detention of debtors. It is situated near the new bank on the south side of the Duke of Gloucester street. Miss Mary L. Foster, in her ''Colonial Capitols,'' discredits its prison associations, as she writes: ''In a description of Williamsburg during Spotswood's time (1710-23), it was said that near the Capitol is a strong, sweet prison for criminals and on the other side of an open court another for debtors.'' This, she continues, ''would place the debtor's prison at the other end of town.''

Bassett Hall.—Formerly the home of Judge Bassett. George Washington was a frequent and welcome visitor here and the Judge was famous throughout the Old Dominion for his hospitality. It was also the home of President John Tyler, in 1841. Thomas Moore, the poet, is said to have composed his poem, ''To the Firefly,'' while sitting on the porch at twilight.

TO THE FIREFLY.

At morning, when the earth and sky
  Are glowing with the light of spring,
We see thee not, thou humble fly!
  Nor think upon thy gleaming wing.

But when the skies have lost their hue,
  And sunny lights no longer play,
Oh, then we see and bless thee, too,
  For sparkling o'er the dreary way.

Thus let me hope, when lost to me
  The lights that now my life illume,
Some milder joys may come, like thee,
  To cheer, if not to warm, the gloom.

The Blair House (South Side of Duke of Gloucester Street).—This was the home of Hon. John Blair, Judge of the United States Supreme Court. Judge Blair was appointed to this office by George Washington. He was Auditor General of Virginia from 1732 to 1771 and vestryman of Bruton Church 1744.

Peyton Randolph House (Francis Street).—This house, built in 1775, still stands intact. A tablet has been placed upon it which reads:

> "Home of Peyton Randolph, Attorney General of Virginia, Speaker of the House of Burgesses, First President of the Continental Congress, Born 1722, Died 1775."

He was Speaker of the House when Patrick Henry made his celebrated speech, "If this be treason"— This patriot lies buried under the Chapel of William and Mary College.

Tazewell Hall (England Street).—The home of Sir John Randolph and Edmund, his nephew. Sir John was Speaker of the House in 1736 and Vestryman of Bruton Church, 1729.

Edmund Randolph was Attorney General 1789-94, Governor of Virginia, 1786-8; Secretary of State, 1794-5. Also Delegate to Congress 1779-82 and Delegate to the Constitutional Convention in 1787.

The First Theater in the United States.—The site of this playhouse is on the southeast corner of Blair Avenue, near the Capitol monument. It was built in 1716, and Miss Johnson describes some of the dramatic scenes enacted in this quaint little theater in her story of "Audrey."

The first company that played in America first appeared here in 1752, under the management of Lewis Hallam, Sr. The orchestra was under the leadership of Mr. Peter Pelham, organist at Bruton Church.

Washington was a frequent attendant at this play-house.

Masonic Temple (Francis Street).—The first grand lodge of Virginia was organized in this house, now dilapidated and in ruins. The present Masonic Lodge has in its possession a carved mahogany chair presented to the lodge by Lord Botetourt, the Colonial Governor. It was used by Washington at his inauguration.

Six Chimney Lot.—On the eastern portion of the Hospital Park formerly stood a mansion occupied by Washington and his- wife during their early married life. There is still standing here a brick building said to have been Martha Washington's kitchen, and an elm tree planted by her own hands.

Site of Raleigh Tavern.—This famous inn stood on the site now occupied by Lane's Store. On a portico over the door stood a metal bust of Sir Walter Raleigh, which is now preserved, with other relics, in the Powder Horn.

Here many a social banquet was held, and here Thomas Jefferson was rejected by Rebecca Burwell. Here in 1769, in the famous Apollo Room, George Washington presented the Burgesses with the ''Non-Importation Agreement,'' drawn up by George Mason. After the House was dissolved by Dunmore in 1774, the Burgesses met here and prepared the way for a general Congress. The building was destroyed by fire in 1859.

Fort Magruder.—About a mile and a half from the town, on the road to Yorktown, can be seen the Confederate entrenchments where the famous battle of Williamsburg was fought, May 5, 1862.

Confederates under Longstreet awaited the Federals

at Fort Magruder, Hooker being the first to be attacked. Kearny arrived just in time to support
Hooker. Hancock succeeded in capturing some
redoubts, but no one seemed in supreme command of
the Federal forces and at night the Confederates retired with a loss of about 1,560, Federal loss 2,200.

A tablet in the Bruton Church reads:

"In memory of
the
Confederate
Soldiers
who fell in the
Battle of Williamsburg,
May the 5th, 1862.
And of those who died of
the wounds received
in the same.
They died for us."

In concluding the description of Williamsburg it is
no more than just to mention the Colonial Inn.
Here, in the spacious parlor and dining room, can be
seen the most complete collection of antiquities and
Colonial furniture in the state, and what makes them
more valuable to their possessor, is the fact that they
were in actual use by his own forbears. The pro-
prietor, Mr. J. B. C. Spencer, is the gentleman who
first conceived the idea of the Jamestown Ter-Cen-
tennial and organized the first committee in its in-
terests.

Carter's Grove.—This beautiful Colonial residence is
seven miles from Williamsburg on the James River.
The grove was originally owned by Col. Robert Carter, known as King Carter, and the mansion was
erected by his grandson in 1722, and was the home
of Rebecca Burwell, whom Jefferson wooed and lost.
During the Revolution, Tarleton's troopers raided the
place and their saber cuts can still be seen on the
banisters of the staircase.

CHAPTER X.

YORKTOWN, ENGLAND'S WATERLOO.

There have been far greater battles fought than those at Yorktown, but no other campaign on American soil was fraught with so many significant results as was the siege of Yorktown—results as far reaching as the events which followed the Battle of Waterloo.

"Yorke Toune" was laid out in 1619, but not

YORKTOWN, AS IT IS TODAY.

legally established until 1705. At the opening of the Revolution, it was quite an important little town, having an extensive sea trade. Today the inhabitants number less than two hundred.

Sept. 27, 1781, the British commenced to cannonade the opposing forces, the American army being a mile distant and the French a mile to the left of the Americans. The siege lasted until October 19, the

YORKTOWN BATTLEFIELD
MONUMENT

firing commencing in earnest on the ninth of October, and continuing with awful intensity until the sixteenth, over three hundred pieces of artillery being incessantly engaged. It is said that the carcasses of six or seven hundred horses could be seen floating down the river every day.

On the sixteenth, the British attempted to escape by crossing the river at Gloucester Point, but a severe storm prevented all the detachments from starting and the attempt was abandoned. The next day, Cornwallis sent out a flag of truce, which resulted in his surrender, October 19.

The Battleground.—The British entrenchments are still very much in evidence, overgrown with broomstraw, the seed of which was brought to this country by the British soldiers in the hay for their horses. In a field near the river, stands a beautiful stone monument bearing the following inscriptions: On the south side:

"At York, on October 19, 1781, after a siege of 19 days by 5,500 American and 7,000 French troops of the line, 3,500 Virginia militia, under command of General Thomas Nelson, and 36 French ships of war, Earl Cornwallis, commander of the British forces at York and Gloucester, surrendered his army, 7,251 officers and men, 840 seamen, 244 cannon and 24 standards, to His Excellency George Washington, commander-in-chief of the combined forces of America and France ; to His Excellency the Comte de Rochambeau, commanding the auxiliary troops of his most Christian majesty in America ; and to His Excellency the Comte de Grasse, commanding in chief the naval reserves of France in Chesapeake."

On the north side of the monument:

"The provisional articles of peace concluded November 30, 1782, and the definite treaty of Peace concluded September 3, 1783, between the United States of America and George III, king of Great Britain and Ireland, declare : His Britannic Majesty acknowledges the said United States, viz., New Hampshire, Massachusetts Bay, Rhode Island and Providence Plantations, Connecticut, New York, New Jersey, Pennsylvania, Delaware, Maryland, Virginia, North Carolina, South Carolina and Georgia, to be free sovereign and independent states."

Place of Surrender.—Oct. 19, 1781, Cornwallis agreed to surrender and at two o'clock in the afternoon, the British army advanced to a field adjoining the town, about half a mile to the east, on the south side of the Hampton road. Cornwallis, unable to bear the ordeal, commissioned Gen. O'Hara to act as his substitute. With colors cased, and drums beating, the British laid down their arms, after a siege of nineteen days, thus closing the long drawn out contest of the brave Colonists for an independent government. A monument has been erected here by Capt. Shaw, of Yorktown, at his own expense.

House Where Articles of Capitulation Were Signed. Nearly a mile from Yorktown is a quaint frame residence, known as the ''Moore House,'' situated on ''Temple Farm.'' In the parlor of this house, the terms of surrender of the British army were drawn up and signed.

The house was built in 1713 and is said to have been Gov. Alexander Spotswood's summer home. The place received its name ''Temple Farm'' because of traces of a round edifice surrounded by a wall which is supposed to have been used as a place of worship and burial ground. Only one legible stone remains, bearing the following inscription:

> ''Mayor William Gooch,
> Dyed October 29th, 1655.
> Within this tomb there doth interred lie,
> No shape, but substance, true nobility;
> Itself though young in years, but twenty-nine,
> Yet graced with nature's Morall and divine.
> The church from him did good participate,
> In counsil rare, fit to adorn a state.''

In a field near the house is another old graveyard and in 1834 Dr. W. Shields, who owned the farm, claimed to have discovered pieces of a gravestone which bore the name of Spotswood, and many are inclined to believe that the governor was buried here.

The Nelson House.—Built 1740. A splendid example of a Colonial residence with spacious halls and rooms. The house is surrounded by an old fashioned garden with a boxwood border. It fronts the river on the main street. It was occupied by Gen. Lafayette on his visit to Yorktown and during the siege by Cornwallis as his headquarters. The gable was struck by three cannon balls and another was

NELSON HOUSE, YORKTOWN.

embedded in the brick wall, while still another entered the dining room, shattering the marble mantel. In this room is a secret panel, connecting two secret rooms with the garret. During the Civil war the house was occupied by the Confederates under General Magruder.

The Nelson house at the edge of the town, during the Revolution, was occupied by British soldiers. The American militia under General Nelson disliked to fire upon the house of their commander, but the gallant General at once offered a reward of five guineas to the soldier who fired the first shot. It was not long before the house was in ruins and hardly a trace of it now remains.

General Nelson was a member of the House of Burgesses, one of the signers of the Declaration of Independence and Governor of Virginia. During the siege of Yorktown, he fed his command at his own expense and later gave his personal security to be added to that of the state when a $2,000,000 credit was to be raised.

Cornwallis' Cave.—About fifty yards from the Nelson House, on a hillside, is a cave excavated by order of Lord Cornwallis. It was used by him as a Council Chamber and probably for protection from the enemy's shells. The cave on the river bank is not the original Cornwallis Cave, although called such.

Swan Tavern.—Originally built in 1722. Located on Main Street. Said to be the oldest one in the state. It was burned during the Civil War. The present building stands upon the original walls.

Custom House.—The oldest and first Custom House in the United States is located here. Built in 1715.

Werowocomoco.—Near Yorktown on the north side of York River, was the home of Powhatan, where Capt John Smith was brought after his capture by that chief. Here occurred the famous Pocahontas incident. Smith wrote that it was "some 14 myles from James Towne."

CHAPTER XI.

A short distance up the James River on the left bank is a quiet little village called Smithfield—the home of the American goober or peanut, a staple crop in Virginia.

Here are large factories and warehouses where the peanuts are purchased from the farmers, cleaned, sorted, polished and prepared for market. The American consumption of peanuts amounts to over 6,000,000 bushels and is valued at over $14,000,000.

The average yield is over twenty bushels per acre. The seeds are planted 8 to 20 inches apart, about two bushels in the pod, being used per acre. They are harvested by plowing, men with pitchforks following the plow and shaking the loosened vines from the earth and piling them in windrows. After lying in the sunshine they are stacked in small shocks and capped with hay. In two or three weeks the peanuts are picked by nomadic gangs of negroes.

The Virginia crop amounts to about 4,000,000 bushels annually, estimated at $2,226,000 value.

St. Luke's Church.—About five miles from Smithfield is the Old Brick Church built in 1632, the oldest building of English construction in America.

The old tower church at Jamestown is of later date and while Bruton at Williamsburg (1683) as an organization is the oldest in America, its present edifice is antedated by St. Luke's, near Smithfield. This edifice was built under the supervision of Joseph Bridges,

father of Gen. Jos. Bridges, "Councellor of State."
The church was partially destroyed by a storm in
1884, and its restoration was undertaken by the Rev.
David Barr.

A most beautiful stained glass window commemor-

ST. LUKE'S CHURCH, SMITHFIELD

ates the landing at Jamestown and the subsequent de-
velopment of the Old Dominion. It is divided into
twelve sections with windows in honor of Washington, Robert E. Lee, James Madison, Sir Walter
Raleigh, John Smith, John Rolfe and other well
known Colonists.

In 1891, during excavations for the burial of Gen. Joseph Bridges, the feet and legs of a lady were found in front of the pulpit. They are believed to be those of Miss Norsworthy, who was buried in the aisle in 1666, over two hundred years ago.

INTERIOR ST. LUKE'S CHURCH, SMITHFIELD

The old pulpit with its sounding board, the old pews and other features of the early church, have been faithfully copied and the interior restored as near like the original as possible. A trip to Smithfield and this historic Church will well repay every visitor to the Jamestown Exposition.

CHAPTER XII.

PETERSBURG, THE CITY OF THE CRATER.

This thriving little city is in Dinwiddie County on the Appomattox River, twenty-three miles south of Richmond. It is the third city in the state in size and importance and was incorporated in 1748. Population, 24,000.

BLANFORD CHURCH, PETERSBURG

During the early settlement of Virginia, God-fearing pioneers erected a line of churches from Norfolk to Petersburg, each ten miles apart. One of the best known of these churches is the one at Petersburg.

Blanford Church.—Bristol Parish was established by

act of the House of Burgesses in 1643. The first
parish church known as the "Chapple," was located
near the Appomattox River in Prince George County,
about two miles below Petersburg. The present
church on Wells Hill was completed in 1737. Its
original form was a rectangle, but in 1752 it was
changed to the form of a T. Services were discontinued in 1781, and for a century, the "old pile" lay
crumbling under the devastating storms of time.

In 1882 the work of restoration commenced under
the auspices of the various patriotic and memorial
associations. During the period (about 1841), when
its walls were slowly crumbling to dust, some unknown
person, evidently under the spell of its associations,
wrote the following poem upon its walls:

Thou art crumbling to the dust, old pile,
    Thou art hastening to thy fall,
And 'round thee in thy loneliness
    Clings the ivy to the wall.
The worshippers are scattered now
    Who knelt before thy shrine,
And silence reigns where anthems rose,
    In days of "Auld Lang Syne."

And sadly sighs the wandering wind
    Where oft, in years gone by,
Prayers rose from many hearts to Him
    The Highest of the High;
The tramp of many a busy foot
    That sought thy aisles is o'er,
And many a weary heart around
    Is still forever more.

How doth ambition's hope take wing,
    How droops the spirit now!
We hear the distant city's din,
    The dead are mute below.
The sun that shone upon their paths
    Now gilds their lonely graves;
The zephyrs which once fanned their brows,
    The grass above them waves.

Oh! could we call the many back
    Who've gathered here in vain—
Who've careless roved where we do now,
    Who'll never meet again;

How would our weary souls be stirred,
  To meet the earnest gaze
Of the lovely and the beautiful,
  The lights of other days.

This poem has been copied, and a tablet containing its verses now hangs upon the wall of the church.

The edifice is now used as a Confederate Memorial Chapel. The church is surrounded by an ancient graveyard, marked by an old brick wall, now a part of the modern cemetery. June the 9th, Confederate Memorial Day services are held at this chapel, which is situated near the battlefield of the Crater. Each of the thirteen Confederate States is to place a memorial window in this edifice, in memory of the soldiers who fell on the Petersburg battlefields. Virginia, Missouri and Louisiana have already installed their memorial. The inscription on the Louisiana window reads:

"To the glorious memory of those brave men of the Washington Artillery, of New Orleans, La., who gave their lives for the Confederate Cause."

The Daughters of the Confederacy have erected a tablet which reads as follows:

In Loving Memory
of
The Citizen Soldiers of Petersburg, the
Gray-Haired Sires and Beardless
Youths, who on
June 9, 1864,
Laid Down Their Lives Near this Venerable Church in Successful Defense
of our Altars and Firesides.

Another tablet is inscribed:

"To the Glory of God and in memory of Virginia Patriots and Heroes of the Confederate Army. "Eternal right, though all fail, can never be made wrong."

Another inscription is:

"In memory of the Patriots who planned, upheld and achieved the Independence of the United States of America, 1775-1782."

The oldest date on the tombstones in the adjoining cemetery is 1702, but it seems to have been a not uncommon custom for the Colonists to have their dead disinterred in England and brought to Virginia for burial, so that many early dates are found on Virginia gravestones that are not accurate indications of the real age of a burial ground.

During the battles of Petersburg, shot and shell shrieked through this city of the dead, striking both the church and many of the tombstones. In the more modern part of the graveyard can still be seen the marks of cannon-balls and shells. Many slabs were splintered into a thousand fragments, while monuments and fences still bear the sacrilegious imprint of death dealing projectiles.

"The Crater."—Some of the most important military operations of the Civil War centered around Petersburg, for Petersburg was the key to Richmond, and Richmond was the capital of the Confederacy. The Federals under Gen. Grant commenced operations here in 1864, and after several unsuccessful attempts to seize the city, siege was begun June 19, 1864. The Confederate position was defended by Gen. Mahone. Gen. Lee had been surprised by Grant's movement upon Petersburg, and many precious hours were lost before he could be convinced that the Federal troops were concentrating upon Petersburg.

The Federals decided to mine the entrenchments and fortifications of the Confederates, and with this end in view, the most elaborate preparations were made. Not the smallest detail was neglected, and the tunnel was completed several hundred feet before the Confederates had their suspicions aroused by the concentration of Federal troops at certain points and their withdrawal from other positions. Even then they were led to believe it could not be possible, as

Grant's army was over five hundred feet from their lines at the nearest point and the longest mine ever constructed was not much over four hundred feet long. It would not be possible, the Confederates argued, to ventilate a tunnel of 500 feet, but by a simple system of box flues and a bonfire to create a draught, the Federals easily overcame that difficulty. Their sus-

BATTLEFIELD OF THE CRATER, PETERSBURG.

picions growing, the Confederates commenced to countermine, but three hundred and seventy-five feet of tunnel were constructed and no Federal mines were discovered.

The best modern machinery of warfare in possession of the Union army was concentrated upon the point where the explosion was to take place. Orders were issued and every detail provided for, so that the troops would charge with the greatest celerity.

July 30, 1864, the main fuse connected with two subsidiary fuses was ignited, but after burning to the main fuse, it went out. Another attempt was made to ignite, this time successfully. Suddenly, without warning, a detachment of Confederate soldiers, numbering 272, were precipitated into the air with terrific violence, destroying a battery and tearing open the earth for 135 feet long, 90 feet wide and 30 feet deep. When the smoke partially cleared away, a vast chasm yawned at the very feet of the Confederate army, while buried in the pit lay nearly three hundred of their comrades.

PEACE MONUMENT, PETERSBURG.

Like clock work the Federal guns boomed forth, and shot and shell fell like hail, but hindered by the unwieldiness of their brigades, the Union forces failed to charge with the alacrity planned and with wonderful bravery the Confederates were able to rally and meet the charge when it did come with decisive success, and here in this awful pit perished scores and hundreds of the gallant boys in blue.

At the Westmoreland Club in Richmond may be seen an oil painting of the Battle of Petersburg, purchased by the Norfolk and Western Railroad Company for $13,000 and presented to Gen. Mahone, the officer in charge of the Confederate troops.

Final operations were commenced against Petersburg, March 25, 1865, and after the battle of Five Forks, March 31 and April 1, it was evacuated April 2 and 3 and surrendered April 3, 1865, completing one of the bloodiest and fiercest campaigns of the war.

Peace Monument.—On the Hare farm, a short distance from Petersburg, 650 of the Maine First Artillery fell in a brave charge upon the Confederate ranks, and this monument has been erected in memory of both the Union and Confederate soldiers who fell here.

The total loss in the battles of Petersburg were as follows: June 15-19, 1864, 11,386; June 20 to 30, 769; July 1 to 31, 1,081; August 1 to 31, 1,077; total 14,313.

CHAPTER XIII.

RICHMOND—THE CITY OF CHIVALRY.

All the romance and chivalry of the Old South centered around Richmond, the capital and the key to the Confederacy, the home of Robert E. Lee and of Jefferson Davis. Its historic associations are still dear to every southern heart.

The Peninsula, the Wilderness, Petersburg, Cold Harbor, Fair Oaks, Gains Mill, Seven Pines and many other battlefields were each deadly milestones on the road to Richmond. "On! on! to Richmond!" became the Federal battle cry, and the city soon became surrounded by walls of fire and fields of carnage—the graveyards of friends and foes, and while death and destruction reigned without, gaunt famine prevailed within, the city finally surrendering to Fate, April 3, 1865.

Today, nearly half a century since these awful scenes were enacted, the bonds of brotherhood and peace have been reunited, but the scars and marks of conflict still remain, sacred shrines for every American, regardless of distinction as to "blue" or "gray," Federal or Confederate.

St. John's Church.—The most important Colonial landmark in Richmond undoubtedly is St. John's Church, where Patrick Henry uttered those memorable words that have echoed down the years with significant intensity: "Give me liberty or give me death!"

There were two early churches in this parish, but their history is somewhat uncertain. The vestry in

1740 decided to erect a church in 1749 on an acre of land donated by William Boyd. The church was surrounded by a graveyard, which for many years was the only one in Richmond. The oldest inscription on the tombstones is 1751, on that of the rector of Albemarle parish, the Rev. Rob't Rose.

The pulpit was in the east end of the church and,

ST. JOHN'S CHURCH, RICHMOND

near the northern wall, between the first row of seats and the chancel, stood Patrick Henry that eventful 20th day of March, 1775.

Concluding his stirring appeal to arms, he said: "Gentlemen may cry, peace, peace—but there is no peace. The war is actually begun! The next gale that sweeps from the north will bring to our ears the clash of resounding arms! Our brethren are already in the field! Why stand we here idle? What is it that gentlemen wish? What would they have? Is life so dear, or peace so sweet, as to be purchased at the price of chains and slavery? Forbid it, Almighty God! I know not what course others may take, but as for me,'' he cried, ''Give me liberty or give me death!''

''No murmur of applause was heard,'' says Wirt, his biographer. ''The effect was too deep. After a trance of a moment, several members started from their seats. The cry 'to arms,' seemed to quiver on

INTERIOR, ST. JOHN'S CHURCH, RICHMOND.

every lip, and gleam from every eye. That super-natural voice still sounded in their ears, and shivered along their arteries.'' And here the visitor still feels the sacred presence of that time-honored patriot.

During the Revolutionary period, regular services were not held in the church, and in 1818 dissension in the parish was caused by the proposal to either remove the church, add to it, or build a new one. A new church was finally decided upon and the corner

stone laid by the Masonic Lodge, but the work was
eventually abandoned. In 1830 an addition was made
to the old church and the interior remodeled.

The Capitol of the Confederacy.—Located on Capitol
Square. This venerable structure has been entirely
remodeled and massive
wings have been added
to it on both sides.
Stately stone steps lead
up to its portals, pre-
senting one of the finest
State Houses in the
country.

Many interesting relics
are p r e s e r v e d here,
among them the Speak-
er's Chair of the House
of Burgesses at Wil-
liamsburg, used when
Patrick Henry made his
celebrated speech, ''If
this be treason—George
the Third can make the
most of it.''

SPEAKER'S CHAIR, HOUSE
OF BURGESSES.

Another Colonial relic is the old stove presented to
the House of Burgesses by Lord Botetourt, Governor
of Virginia. It was made in London in 1770 by
Buzaglo, a celebrated stovemaker of that period, and
was called by him a ''warming machine.'' Before it
was completed the Governor died, but his heirs and
executor, the Duke of Beaufort, carried out his purpose and forwarded it to the Colony.

Capitol Square.—At one corner of the square stands
an old-fashioned building surmounted by a cupola,

called the "Bell Tower." From this tower, the Confederates surveyed the surrounding country on the lookout for the approach of Federal troops. Opposite the State House is an exquisite life size equestrian statue of Gen. George Washington, who was born in Virginia in 1732 and died at Mt. Vernon, Va., Dec. 14, 1799. In the center court of the State House is another beautiful marble statue of Washington done by the noted sculptor, Houdon, said to be the only one made of this famous soldier, patriot and statesman from life. So lifelike is it that the tourist stands entranced, waiting almost for the marble figure to move. It is said that France has offered the City of Richmond $100,000 for this almost priceless work.

HOUSE OF BURGESSES STOVE.

The Home of Gen. Robert E. Lee.—Now occupied by the Virginia Historical Society and used as a museum of Confederate relics. Records, books, maps, portraits and war relics here abound and the tourist or student of history cannot afford to neglect visiting the home of this celebrated general.

Libby Prison.—The site where this Confederate prison was located is now occupied by the Crystal Ice Company, the original building having been removed to the World's Fair at Chicago. Belle Isle, the Confederate prison for Confederate soldiers, is an island in the James River, accessible from Richmond by electric cars.

Hollywood.—The Confederate Cemetery. Here lie entombed the remains of Mr. Jefferson Davis, the President of the Confederacy, and by his side sleeps his wife, who died in October, 1906. On Gettysburg Hill is a monument to Gen'l Geo. E. Pickett.

Other Historic Landmarks.—The Soldiers' Home for Confederate Soldiers is located in the western part of the city. A confectionery store on Broad and Ninth Streets marks the building where the Confederacy printed its money. The Woman's College, Male Orphan Asylum, City Alms House, Seabrook's Ware House and Chimborazo Hospitals, were each used as asylums for the sick and wounded soldiers during the war. The Confederate Treasury and office of Jefferson Davis were located in the post-office building. The Tredegar Iron Works, where the material for the Confederate Army was manufactured, is still running.

CHAPTER XIV.

BATTLEFIELDS NEAR RICHMOND.

"On Fame's eternal Camping Ground
Their silent tents are spread,
While glory guards with solemn round
The bivouac of the dead."

Cold Harbor.—Nine miles northeast of Richmond in Hanover Co., near the Chickahominy River. June 27, 1862, a battle took place here between McClellan and Lee's forces and again on June 2 to 4, 1864, between Gen. Grant and Gen. Lee, ending the 30-day campaign of the Wilderness. Grant with 80,000 men threw himself upon Lee's entrenchments, but was repulsed in less than an hour with a loss of 6,000 men. The Confederate loss was less than 2,000. This battlefield has been converted into a cemetery where thousands of men are buried in trenches.

Chester.—Between Richmond and Petersburg. May 6-7, 1864. Total loss 100. Fifteen miles south of the city.

Chaffin's Bluff.—Sept. 28, 1864. Total loss, 3,330. Entrenchments can still be seen. Boat can be taken on James River or it can be reached by carriage.

Dutch Gap.—In order to make an attack on the Confederates, Gen'l Butler cut a canal across the country for eight miles connecting the river at the bend. See map, page 106.

Darbytown.—Oct. 7, 1864, Gen'ls Sherman and Johnson in command. Total loss 458; 5 m. from Richmond.

Drewry's Bluff.—May 12, 1864. Total loss, 2,506. Eight miles south of the city.

Ellerson's Mill.—Part of the "Seven Days" fight. Seven miles from Richmond.

Ft. Harrison.—Visited by President Lincoln July

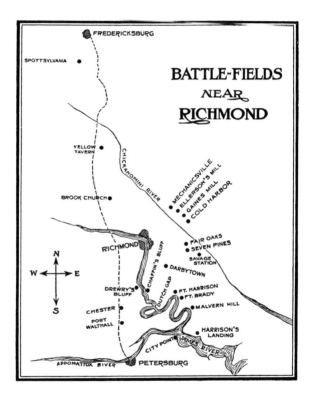

8, 1862. Eighty-five thousand Federal troops were stationed here at that time. A National Cemetery is located here.

Fair Oaks.—(A mile and a half from Seven Pines.) May 3, 1862, the battle of Seven Pines originated here.

Gaines Mill.—(Eight miles northeast of Richmond.) June 27, 1862. This battle was a continuation of that at Mechanicsville, McClellan's forces being attacked by those of Gen. Lee, the former's loss being nearly 7,000 and the Confederates' about seven hundred more.

Mechanicsville.—(Seven miles northeast of Richmond.) June 26, 1862. Part of the "Seven Days' Battle." See **Gaines Mill.** A part of McClellan's army under Fitz John Porter was attacked here by Longstreet and Hill.

Savage Station.—(Ten miles east of Richmond.) June 29, 1862. Part of the Seven Days' Battle between Gen. McClellan and Gen. Lee's forces. Abandoned by Union forces with its hospital containing 2,500 sick and wounded. Total loss nearly 1,600.

Seven Pines.—(Seven miles east of Richmond.) May 31 and June 1, 1862, Federal and Confederate forces engaged. Each numbered about 45,000. Union loss 5,031; Confederate, 6,134. Gen. J. E. Johnson in charge of Confederate forces, was wounded and replaced by G. W. Smith. McClellan was in charge of the Federal troops. This battle was commenced at Fair Oaks, and was one of the Seven Days' fight around Richmond and the first great conflict between the Confederate Army of Northern Virginia and the Federal Army of the Potomac.

A National Cemetery is located here and out of 1,380 graves only 162 are identified.

"**Yellow Tavern.**"—May 11, 1864. Total loss, 259.

CHAPTER XV.

ALEXANDRIA, THE HOME OF WASHINGTON AND LEE.

Christ Church.—Started 1767, completed 1773, for six hundred pounds sterling. A tax of 31,185 pounds of tobacco was levied upon the parish for this purpose. The exterior is typically Colonial and the edifice was designed by James Wren. Pew number five was

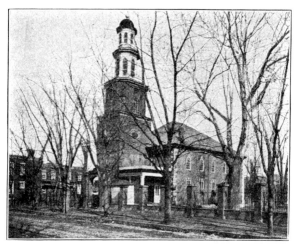

CHRIST CHURCH, ALEXANDRIA.

purchased by George Washington. Rev. Townsend Dale was the first rector. One peculiar custom of the early church was the employment of women for ushers and sextons.

Here in this building, one morning after service, George Washington publicly advised withdrawing allegiance from King George. The high backed pews have all been cut down with the exception of Washington's, which still remains as it was in Colonial days. It is marked by a silver plate, as is the one formerly occupied by Gen. Robt. E. Lee. During the war the church was seized by the Federal authorities, but restored after peace had been declared. On each side of the chancel are mural tablets, one in honor of Washington and the other in memory of Robt. E. Lee.

Foreign Sovereigns During the Colonial Period.

	Spain.	France.	England.
1578...	Philip II.	Henry III.	Elizabeth.
1589...	Philip II.	Henry IV.	Elizabeth.
1602...	Philip III.	Henry IV.	Elizabeth.
1603...	Philip III.	Henry IV.	James I.
1621...	Philip IV.	Louis XIII.	James I.
1627...	Philip IV.	Louis XIII.	Charles I.
1643...	Philip IV.	Louis XIV.	Charles I.
1651...	Philip IV.	Louis XIV.	Cromwell.
1662...	Philip IV.	Louis XIV.	Charles II.
1665...	Charles II.	Louis XIV.	Charles II.
1686...	Charles II.	Louis XIV.	James II.
1689...	Charles II.	Louis XIV.	William & Mary.
1699...	Charles II.	Louis XIV.	Anne.
1701...	Philip V.	Louis XIV.	Anne.
1715...	Philip V.	Louis XV.	George I.
1729...	Philip V.	Louis XV.	George II.
1748...	Ferdinand VI.	Louis XV.	George II.
1760...	Charles III.	Louis XV.	George III.
1774...	Charles III.	Louis XVI.	George III.
1776...	Charles III.	Louis XVI.	George III.

CHAPTER XVI.

The history of the early church in America is closely woven into the political fabric of the nation.

The first white child born in America was baptized on Roanoke Island in 1587 by a chaplain of Raleigh's Colony. The first church service was celebrated by "Good Maister Hunt" at Jamestown in 1607. The first legislative Assembly, the House of Burgesses, was organized by Churchmen and met in the church at Jamestown. Robt. Livingston, who led the opposition to the Stamp Act, was a Churchman. Patrick Henry, the patriotic orator; Peyton Randolph, President of the first Continental Congress; Geo. Washington, Commander-in-Chief of the army; Richard Henry Lee, who introduced the resolution of Independence in the second Continental Congress; Thomas Jefferson, who drafted the Declaration, and thirty-five of the men who signed it, were all Churchmen. Franklin, Hamilton and Madison, with a host of other patriots and leaders, were identified with the church and during Colonial days, we find the vestrymen exercising semi-political powers. Aside from the more important Colonial churches that have already been described, the following edifices will well repay any one who cares to visit these sacred shrines:

Old Falls Church.—(Fairfax County. Truro Parish.) Built about 1734. Rebuilt 1769. Truro Parish. Cost $3,000. Washington was a member of the vestry in 1763, and also George Mason, author of the "Bill of

Rights.'' The churchyard is said to have been the camping ground of Braddock's Army and the building was occupied by soldiers during the Revolution, and by the Federal troops during the Civil War. A long list of distinguished names are recorded as ministers and communicants at this sacred shrine. Efforts are now being made to complete its entire restoration.

Pohick.—(Mount Vernon. Truro Parish.) The parish church of George Washington and George Mason. The first record in the vestry book is dated 1732. The first minister was Rev. Lawrence de Butts. Washington's father was vestryman in 1735. George Mason became warden in 1749. On October 25, 1762, George Washington was elected vestryman. It is said Washington drew the plan of the present church in 1769. Like other Virginia churches, the edifice suffered much during the Civil War. In 1874 it was repaired and renovated and consecrated in October, 1875. The entire restoration is now in progress.

Aquia Church.—(Stafford Co.) Founded about 1664. Rev. John Waugh, probably the first rector. A communion service of three pieces of beaten silver donated to the church by Rev. Mr. Alexander Scott, A. M., 1739, is still in use by the church, and during the wars of the Revolution, the War of 1812 and the Civil War, they were buried for safe keeping.

The present church was erected 1757 on the site of one built in 1751, which was destroyed by fire. Over the east door is the following inscription in white letters:

''Built A. D. 1751. Destroyed by fire 1751, and rebuilt A. D. 1757 by Mourning Richards, Undertaker, Wm. Copeirs, Mason.'' In 1837 the building was in ruins, but was restored before the war. During the

Civil War it was used by soldiers and again almost destroyed, but once more restored.

St. Peter's Church.—(New Kent Co.) Probably founded about 1656. Rev. John Ball was the rector in 1686. The present church was built about 1703. The Rev. David Mossom was minister for forty years, and was considered a quaint old character, especially noted for his temper. He married Geo. Washington and Martha Custis at the White House on the Pamunkey River, a few miles from the church. He died 1767. The church is located near Turnstall's Station, 20 miles east of Richmond.

Hungar's Church.—(Northampton Co.) Seven miles north of Eastville. Built about 1690 and in actual use for more than 200 years. First minister Rev. William Cotton (1635). The Communion Set used by the lower Hungar Church was presented by John Custis of Williamsburg, and is now in use by Christ Church, Eastville.

Christ Church.—(Eastville, Northampton Co.) Built about 1826. The Communion Set used by this church bears the inscription:

"Ex dono Francis Nicholson,"
Lieut. Governor of Virginia, 1690-2.

Christ Church.—(Lancaster Co.) Built 1732. The parish was organized prior to 1654, as Rev. Thos. Sax was the recorded minister at that date. The first church on the present site was built 1670. The famous Col. Robert Carter, known as King Carter, paid for the erection of the new building in 1732, the entire north cross of the building being reserved for his **family.** He was buried in the churchyard, where his tomb can still be seen. The walls of the church are three feet thick. There are twenty-five pews, three of which, designed for the Carter family, will contain twenty persons each.

Vauter's Church.—(Essex Co.) St. Anne's Parish. Built about 1714. Earliest recorded minister was Rev. John Bagge, 1724. A cruciform brick building. Its windows are guarded by solid wooden shutters. The church stands in a grove of walnut and oak and is a venerable landmark in this part of the country.

Among other historic churches are the following:

Abingdon Church.—(Gloucester Co.) About 15 miles from Jamestown. A Register bearing date 1677 is still in existence. In this territory occurred the Pocahontas incident, so tradition claims. In the first church located here worshipped Mildred Warner, grandmother of George Washington. The present building is supposed to have been built in 1755.

St. Paul's Church.—(King George Co.) Erected about 1750.

The Fork Church.—(Hanover Co.) Built 1735. Here Patrick Henry was baptised when an infant and here his cousin Dorothea, later Dolly Madison, worshipped.

The complete history of Virginia's Colonial churches would fill a large volume.

PART II.

THE EXPOSITION IN BRIEF.

Opened April 26, 1907. **Closes** November 30, 1907. Gates open 8 a. m. Close, 11 p. m. Government buildings, 9 a. m. to 6 p. m.

Admission.—Adults, 50 cents; children, 25 cents.

Powhatan Guards.—Constitutes the police force of 100 men.

Grounds.—Cover 400 acres, located on Hampton Roads, five miles from Norfolk City limits, four from Old Point Comfort and five from Newport News. The grounds have three miles of water front.

Lee's Parade.—A beautiful plaza comprising many acres, partially surrounded by the Exposition Palaces, nearly half a mile wide and a mile long. Here military evolutions will take place, forming a gorgeous spectacle seldom ever witnessed.

Plan.—Stretching along the historic waters of Hampton Roads for three miles, the Exposition presents an unusual spectacle of beauty and splendor. The style of architecture is Colonial, the buildings low in height, but covering an immense area of space. White, yellow and red are the prevailing colors. The key to the Exposition plan lies within the confines of Commonwealth avenue. The Administration Building forms the center of the mammoth palaces. It faces the Lagoons and Raleigh Square, giving a fine view of the Grand Basin and the Government Piers. Along the water front are the State Buildings and entering the main gate, directly to the left, is the **War Path.**

The principal palaces are as follows:

Administration Building.—160x236 feet. Located on Pocahontas street, opposite the Lagoons. A Colonial structure of red brick and concrete designed for permanent use. The principal Exposition building. The center building is the Auditorium and is connected by colonnades with the History Building on the east and the Educational and Social Economy Building on the west, each of which covers 124x129 feet.

Food Products Building.—250x300 feet. On Pocahontas street and Commonwealth avenue, and Gilbert street. Here elaborate displays of food stuffs will be on exhibition. Machinery used in the preparation of food stuffs will be shown in actual operation.

Mines and Metallurgy.—100x250 feet. A beautiful Colonial structure of permanent construction on Pocahontas street and Commonwealth avenue, opposite the Machinery and Transportation Building. Here may be found specimens of coal, gold, silver, copper, iron, marble, onyx, building stone and other minerals from the crude ore to the finished products.

Machinery and Transportation Building.—280x550 feet. Situated on Pocahontas street and Commonwealth avenue. Separated from the Liberal Arts Building by the Lagoon. In this structure may be seen the carriage presented to Lafayette by the United States government; also the state coach used by President Lincoln the night of his assassination. Steel Pullman coaches, railroad trains, machinery and mechanical devices of all descriptions are exhibited in this handsome palace.

States' Exhibit Palace.—300x500 feet. The type of architecture of this structure, like all the other pal-

aces, is Colonial. It faces Lee's Parade on Commonwealth avenue. Along the facade appear the names
of the states having special exhibits within this building. Fruits, vegetables, grains, woods, minerals and
a host of other products are displayed in profusion.

Manufactures and Liberal Arts Building.—280x550
feet. Pocahontas street, Commonwealth avenue and
Powhatan street. A permanent structure of Colonial
style. Here may be seen a varied display of manufactures, books and publications. Laird & Lee's booth,
section 28, contains an exhibit of the firm's many
books, including the famous series of Webster's New
Standard Dictionaries, adopted for use in the schools
of many leading cities and awarded Gold Medal at
the St. Louis and Portland Expositions.

Arts and Crafts Village.—Iron Shop, 48x50 feet.

Copper, Silver and Wood Shop.—44x137 feet.

Textile Building.—53x88 feet.

Mothers' and Children's Building.—60x100 feet.
Willoughby boulevard and Bacon street.

Model School.—35x45 feet.

Pottery Building.—48x50 feet.

Pocahontas Hospital.—50x85 feet.

Hall of Congress.—236x160 feet.

Army and Navy Building.—Powhatan street and
Commonwealth avenue.

Negro Building.—250x150 feet. Maryland avenue.

Palaces of Commerce.—Entrance to War Path.

Marine Appliances.—Opposite Mines and Metallurgy
Building.

Power and Alcohol Building.—Near Lee's Parade.

Grand Piers.—2,400 feet long, 800 feet wide, connected by cross piers, 1,200 feet long, at a distance
of 2,400 feet from shore, forming a water basin in the

center of 40 acres. Cost $400,000. Built by the government.

Government Buildings.—Facing the Grand Basin. Separated from each other by Raleigh Square. Two center buildings represent the Fisheries Building and Smithsonian Building. The Navy, Army, Postoffice, Agricultural, State, Treasury and other departments are well represented in these structures.

STATE BUILDINGS AND EXHIBITS.

The State Buildings are located along the shore line, on Willoughby boulevard, and the Main Exposition Palaces in the center of the grounds in front of Lee's Parade. The government structures face the piers, and the Arts and Crafts Buildings are east of the Parade Grounds.

The following states have made appropriations or have provided funds by special subscription and many of the buildings provided for have been completed.

Alabama, $25,000; Arkansas, $15,000; Connecticut, $70,000; Delaware, $10,000; Georgia, $50,000; Illinois, $25,000; Kentucky, $40,000; Louisiana, $15,000; Maryland, $65,000; Michigan, $20,000; Missouri, $40,000; Massachusetts, $50,000; New Jersey, $75,000; North Dakota, $15,000; New York, $150,000; North Carolina, $55,000; Ohio, $75,000; Pennsylvania, $100,000; Rhode Island, $50,000; South Carolina, exhibit, $20,000; Virginia, $450,000; Vermont, $10,000; New Hampshire, $10,000; West Virginia, $55,000.

Arkansas.

Arkansas will be represented in the States' Exhibit Palace.

Alabama.

Alabama appropriated $25,000 for an exhibit. Cotton and iron are exploited, while timber **and** other products come in for their share in the display. A part of the exhibit is the mammoth iron statue of Vulcan, from Birmingham.

California.

Los Angeles has an exhibit of pictures, samples of every kind of fruits and vegetables raised in Southern California, exhibits of the different industries and manufactories.

Connecticut.

Connecticut has reproduced the famous Benjamin Talmage home, located at Litchfield, which was the first Colonial mansion erected in Connecticut. The owner was intrusted with the execution of Major Andre, the British spy, and in this house were planned many of the successful campaigns of the Revolution. The great entrance has its walls finished in soft old Venetian red and furnished in pieces of the seventeenth century. In the drawing room is a choice collection of furniture of the eighteenth century, including very fine mirrors of Washington design. Queen Anne and Chippendale sofa, covered in an ancient flowered pattern, will be noticeable. The tea room is ''Empire,'' the treatment being yellow with a rare set of First Empire furniture.

Delaware.

Delaware, the ''Diamond State,'' has a building of Colonial hip-roofed design with a parquet gallery running around both interior and exterior, the Delaware coat-of-arms over the doorway and the word ''Delaware'' impressed upon the side wall. With Colonial porches, old-time cornices and immense brick chimneys at each end of the building, it is an exceedingly attractive and creditable building.

Florida.

Florida will have an exhibit of fruit and flowers and also an historical collection. Wide attention is being attracted in floricultural circles and from scientists making a special study of flower-breeding, to the pollen collection, invented by Prof. E. Moulie of Jacksonville. Professor Moulie will exhibit his various perfumes, surrounded by the flowers from which they are made, and with each step in the process illustrated.

Georgia.

The Georgia Building is a representation of "Bulloch Hall," at Rosewell, Georgia. "Bulloch Hall" was the home of Mattie Bulloch, mother of President Roosevelt, and here she was married to the President's father. The reproduction of this building typifies several periods in the history of the Empire State of the South. The builder of the house was second Governor of Georgia; Archibald Bulloch, the President's uncle, was a captain in the Confederate navy, and his brother, James, was an officer in Lee's army. The twelve rooms of this building will be furnished by the leading cities of the state, including Atlanta, Savannah, Columbia, Macon, Valdosta, Waycross, Statesboro, Albany and Cordele. The state appropriated the sum of $50,000 for an exhibit at the Jamestown Exposition and the funds for the erection of the building have been raised by popular subscription. The State Building fronts on Willoughby boulevard and the waters of Hampton Roads and is a handsome structure of Colonial architecture.

Illinois.

Illinois has a beautiful Colonial building of pressed brick veneer, with stall trimmings, with wide porches and verandas. The main reception hall is a feature of the attractiveness of the Illinois Building, with its immense fireplace, broad stairs and spacious window seats, giving the entire building an air of hospitality. The walls of the reception room are decorated with the Lincoln Exhibit, now in the hands of the Historical Society, at Springfield. Illinois will make quite an exhibit in her state building, but space in the other structures has also been filled with exhibits illustrative of the industries of the state.

Indiana.

Indiana is endeavoring to secure funds by popular subscription for an exhibit in historical and educational lines. Some of the large manufacturing industries of the state have exhibits.

Kentucky.

Kentucky has rebuilt Daniel Boone's fort in a grove of stalwart pines in the northwestern corner of the Exposition grounds, the logs for the construction of the same being shipped from various sections of the "Blue Grass State," some of them from the site of the original fort at Boonesboro. There are two main buildings, each twenty feet square, and connected by a roof twenty feet wide. The building has a twenty foot veranda running the full length of each side. Four cabins, each twenty feet square, are erected in addition. These will be used as offices and probably for exhibit purposes.

Louisiana.

Louisiana State Building is 46 by 59 feet in size, two stories in height and of Colonial architecture. It has a 15-foot gallery in front, with eight columns and a similar gallery on the side. The front of the building is almost entirely of glass. Special effort will be made to make a very striking exhibit of the rice, sugar and cotton industry and of the forestry, mineral and oyster resources of Louisiana. The sugar exhibit will consist of samples of sugar canes, a wax model of a cane field, with miniature laborers in the act of cutting the stalks, and miniature cane field implements. A lifelike wax model of the cotton plant, showing the leaves, flowers, pods and open bolls, in addition to stalks of the genuine cotton plants of the most promising varieties grown in the state, with seed cottons, lint cottons, cotton seed products, such as hulls, meals, cake and fertilizers; cotton oils, crude and refined; lard substitutes, cotton goods, cotton stalk paper, together with a model cotton gin and photos of cotton fields are on exhibition.

New Jersey.

The New Jersey State Building fronts on Matoaka place and the Boulevard. It is a stately structure of pure Colonial architecture. The building is two stories in height, and is said to be a replica of General Washington's headquarters at Morristown. The cost was $26,000.

North Dakota.

The site of the North Dakota Building is in the midst of those selected by Virginia, Maryland, Ohio and Pennsylvania, and commands a beautiful view of the Hampton Roads. The lot is 50 by 165 feet and the attractive building is located with a view of being easy of access to all parts of the grounds, as well as having a clear outlook upon the great body of water beyond. The building is completely furnished and has a delightful reception room, 20 by 40 feet, with all modern conveniences.

North Carolina.

The "Old North State" has produced a fine Colonial residence, with large columns and ample porches in front. The interior is of North Carolina yellow pine furniture finish and the furnishings throughout are from North Carolina furniture and textile factories. The appropriation of this state was $55,000 for building and exhibit, besides $5,000 for an exhibit by the colored race of the state.

New York.

New York has a large Colonial mansion at the water's very edge. It is modeled from ''Arlington,'' the Lee homestead across the Potomac from the city of Washington, and is surmounted by a dome resembling that which adorns the Congressional Library at Washington. The building is to cost $31,500, and is located in one of the most advantageous positions on the grounds. The Colonial Dames of the Empire State have brought together a wonderful collection of antiques and relics. Slippers worn by a Colonial belle at her wedding; queer school books, out of which the children learned their lessons; state papers over which the makers of the Republic bent their powdered heads; silver dishes, silhouettes and pictures, historical documents, newspapers, etc.

New Hampshire.

This building is a reproduction of the one erected by Governor Langdon in 1784 and occupied by him until his death, in 1819. Langdon was one of the great New Hampshire men and ranks high among the heroes of the Revolution. He was one of the first senators and also had the distinction of being the first president pro tem of the United States senate. The New Hampshire Colonial Dames of America have contributed an exhibit to the Jamestown Exposition, among which are pottery, valuable pieces of old furniture, a traveling case of solid mahogany filled with cut glass, bottles and glasses, these having been the property of Colonel Cilley before the Revolution; also a miniature of Brig. Gen. Enoch Poor, old fans, laces, old prints, manuscripts and costumes. Among the latter is a piece of the wedding dress of the wife of Governor Tristan Cossyn, who was one of the early governors of that period.

Missouri.

Missouri has provided a fine Colonial structure. The building is of red brick, with its stately porticos and verandas. This stately mansion presents a singular aspect of dignity and repose combined. In appearance it is not unlike the Virginia Building. Colonial in design, it lacks the boldness of execution involved in that type, its severity being tempered with an elaborate profuseness of ornamentation quite fascinating to the artistic contemplation.

Michigan.

Michigan has an appropriation of $20,000, and will have a building on Bennett Circle. The state will have an extensive agricultural, horticultural and forestry exhibit. (See map on page 2.)

Maryland.

Maryland reproduced as her building at the Jamestown Exposition the home of Charles Carroll of Carrollton. Carroll was one of the signers of the Declaration of Independence and survived all the others by half a dozen years. One room of the building is a replica of the old senate chamber at Annapolis, where Washington resigned his commission as Commander-in-Chief of the army. The building has a length of 240 feet. The main building is 70 by 64 feet, the reproduction of the senate chamber 40 by 36 feet, and the entrance hall 25 by 38 feet. A dozen rooms are provided for the convenience of the visitors.

Massachusetts.

Massachusetts has attempted a reproduction of the old State House, as it stands at the head of State street, Boston. The structure is one of the most interesting and quaint in the group of State Buildings. The first story is given over to the entrance and exhibit halls, the circular staircase hall, the old stairway being reproduced faithfully; the commission's offices, curator's room, lavatories, etc. The main feature of the second story is an exact reproduction of the famous old council chamber where James Otis warred against Writs of Assistance, and the Representatives' hall, the scene of so many stirring events. There is the historic balcony, the exterior as it was in Colonial days, the whole surmounted by the lion and the unicorn. The historical collection from Massachusetts is valued at more than $100,000. The articles comprising this collection were all in use in Massachusetts families prior to the time of the Revolution, and the exhibit is, therefore, distinctively Colonial.

Ohio.

Ohio has reproduced in cement block a model of "Adena," the first stone house erected west of the Alleghany mountains, and for several years the home of Governor Worthington, when the capital of the state was at Chillicothe. The furnishings of the house are faithful to the times when the house was built. A fire-proof section contains the $25,000 archæological exhibit of Ohio.

Oklahoma.

This new addition to the Union of States will be well represented at the Exposition with exhibits from her fertile farms, abundant orchards and flourishing gardens. Funds are being subscribed for a building also, and notwithstanding the fact that its first legislature has not been elected a site at the Exposition has been engaged. The site selected is in the western portion of the grounds.

Oregon.

Forty pretty young women from Oregon will come to the Exposition dressed in Indian garb. The scheme is one of the most novel yet suggested for the Exposition. It is proposed to select forty of the most comely women in the state of Oregon and send them on a tour of the United States. They will be dressed in Indian costume, and will advertise the state of Oregon. Their trip will include a three weeks' stay at the Exposition. The party will be at the Exposition either in July or August.

Pennsylvania.

Pennsylvania has constructed a replica of old Independence Hall of Philadelphia. A mammoth four-face electric illumination clock ornaments the tower and all the lines of the tower will be illuminated by rows of electric lights. Original buildings of the University of Pennsylvania will be shown in miniature by a unique model.

Rhode Island.

The Rhode Island Building is a replica of the first capitol of that state. Rhode Island State day will be on the anniversary of the battle of Lake Erie, Tuesday, September 10.

South Carolina.

South Carolina will expend her entire appropriation on an exhibit. The exhibit will be arranged under the heads of agriculture, forestry, Clemson College, cotton manufactures, undeveloped water powers, mineral waters, historical, general manufactures and minerals. The tea exhibit from this state will be very complete, the United States Department of Agriculture having agreed to turn over its exhibit to the South Carolina exhibit, and this exhibit will be supplemented by photographs, bottled goods in all shapes, plants, etc., and, taken as a whole, the tea exhibit will be very complete. South Carolina has been given a space in the States' Exhibit Building, 214 by 18 feet, and has been placed on the artistic installation of the exhibits to make them attractive and spectacular. A large relief map of Charleston harbor is a part of the exhibit. "South Carolina Day" is June 28.

Virginia.

Virginia presents a beautiful type of Colonial architecture. The building has a frontage of 116 feet, including the side porches. It is of brick, with stone and marble ornamentation. The front elevation presents the harmonious effects of Ionic elegance combined with Doric simplicity. Lofty Corinthian columns surmounted with Acanthus leaf capitals support the roof projection above an imposing entrance. The building is designed for reception and entertaining only.

Vermont.

Vermont is constructing a model summer home, a feature for which the "Green Mountain State" is becoming noted. It will be about 24 by 34 feet in dimensions and a story and a half high. The lower floor will be one room, set apart to receive visitors, and will be finished in hard pine and furnished appropriately. A broad piazza will face Hampton Roads. A writing room and toilet rooms will occupy the upper floor. Vermont will have exhibits in marble, slate, granite building stone, maple sugar and syrups, pure foods, dairy products, fruits, fish and game.

West Virginia.

The West Virginia Building has a fine location on the Boulevard. It has a brick foundation, frame superstructures, built on the old Colonial plan, with porches and columns in front and on the sides and terraces connecting the porches. Near the building will be an obelisk of West Virginia coal, 40 by 40 feet at the base and 160 feet high. It will be laid in obelisk form, a strata for each county of the state, and illuminated by electric lights, forming an exhibit visible far out to sea. A large space in the States' Exhibit Palace has been secured for a display of the products of the "Little Mountain State." In the Historic Relic Building will be placed that part of the collection which pertains to the Burr-Blennerhassett conspiracy, James Rumsey's steamboat and John Brown's insurrection, with such other material as is illustrative of that part of the state's history which is of national world-wide importance. Among the articles exhibited is the pack saddle used a hundred years ago in carrying salt from Winchester to Clarksburg, the large spinning wheel, the reel, winding blade, reeds, the little flax spinning wheel, the flax brake, scutching knife and scutching block implements used in making the jeans, linsey linen and tow linen, which clothed the West Virginia pioneers in the infant days of the Republic.

THE WAR PATH.

What the Midway was to Chicago, the Pike to the Louisiana Purchase Exposition and the Trail to the Lewis and Clark Exposition, the War Path is to the Jamestown Exposition.

A few of the more important concessions are as follows:

Freil Lift.—What the Eiffel Tower was to Paris, and the Ferris Wheel to Chicago, the Freil Lift will be to Jamestown. It looks much like a windmill, with airships attached to the arms, and while the arms are going around the upright on which they turn is also going around.

Fair Japan.—A typical street scene, such as would be found in Tokio. The street is lined with little shops and natives are selling their wares. A native theater and restaurant will show the Japs in their histrionic and gastronomic life. A Tea Garden will be sure to entice the passerby. There is a pagoda here and various other things Japanese in architecture, such as bridges and bazaars.

Old Williamsburg.—Colonial Virginia will be presented in a building which will be a copy of the old House of Burgesses in Williamsburg. A moving picture drama in which the old worthies will appear in characteristic costume. Leading and dramatic incidents will be incorporated and the production, it is said, will be of genuine historic and artistic interest.

Old Mill.—The Old Virginia Corn Cracker has been transferred from up in the mountains of West Virginia. It has the overshot wheel and will be seen in operation in picturesque surroundings. Meal will be ground out while you wait and ''Mammies'' will serve hoe cake, batter bread and corn bread with syrup and you can eat country sausages and the real Smithfield ham.

Beautiful Orient will take you through the Land of Egypt. You can ride the camel and buy of the natives. You will see the quaint river craft of the Nile and hear the weird music of the Lotus Land.

Old Jamestown reproduced will appeal particularly to Virginians, and there one may rest and also eat modern cooking on a roof garden overlooking the ancient settlement.

"101 Ranch," a great wild west show. The Miller Brothers, of Oklahoma, are bringing their full outfit and life on the plains will be seen as it is today and as it was when the Indians were rough. The Indians who will come with the ranch, and the cowboys and cowgirls and the Mexicans will number five hundred and there will be a big herd of buffalo and wild Texan steers, with bronchos and rough riders and many special features that one will long remember.

Bostock's Animals.—Bostock will have his American show, which has wintered in Richmond, and his Paris show, just brought over from the Hippodrome, combined, and the wonderful performances of his trained wild animals will be seen at Pine Beach not far from the entrance to the grounds.

The Philippine Reservation will show life as it is among the civilized and Christianized Filipinos and also the rude life in huts of the less civilized natives at work fashioning implements of war or domestic life. Representatives of the War Department have been at work in the islands getting the material and people for this part of the Exposition and the promise is made that it will offer better opportunity for studying the Filipinos than did the exhibit at St. Louis.

OTHER ATTRACTIONS ARE

Temple of Mirth.

Fairy Land.

Baby Incubator.

Hale's Tours.

Paul Revere's Ride.

Trixie, the Educated Horse.

Destruction of San Francisco.

Shooting the Chutes.

Merrimac and Monitor Battle.
Battle of Manassas.
Unknown Regions.
Revolving Parachute.
Esquimaux Village.
Haunted Castle.
Empire of India.
Lee and his Generals.

NAVAL DISPLAY.

Never in the history of the world has there been such an array of battleships as can be seen on the

THE BATTLESHIP VIRGINIA.

historic waters of Hampton Roads. For several miles these mighty monsters are stretched out in a straight line, extending from Old Point to Newport News. Each ship lies 300 yards apart and no one can look upon these beautiful cruisers and battleships without a feeling of pride. Painted a clear white with yellow turrets and funnels they form a picture that cannot be described. In a line of honor before the American fleet under Admiral Evans ride the grim war dogs of the foreign powers, while protecting the entire fleet an outer fringe of torpedo boat destroyers may be seen. Admiral Harrington, of Norfolk, is in charge of the evolutions. Some fifty war vessels are anchored in Hampton Roads; their names and classes are given as follows:

LIST OF SHIPS ATTENDING EXPOSITION.

American.

FIRST-CLASS BATTLESHIPS.

Admiral Evans' flagship is the Connecticut.

	Guns.		Guns.
Connecticut	24	Illinois	18
Louisiana	24	Kearsarge	22
Missouri	20	Kentucky	22
Virginia	24	Ohio	20
Georgia	24	Indiana	16
New Jersey	24	Iowa	18
Rhode Island	24	Minnesota	24
Alabama	18	Maine	20

SECOND-CLASS BATTLESHIP.

Texas, 8 guns.

CRUISERS.

St. Louis, 14 guns. First-class protected cruiser.
Tennessee, 20 guns. Armored.
Washington, 20 guns. Armored.
Cleveland, 10 guns. Third-class protected.
Denver, 10 guns. Third-class protected.
Brooklyn, 20 guns. First-class armored.

MONITORS.

Miantonomah, 9 guns.
Canonicus. Old type.

DESTROYERS.

Hopkins, Hull, MacDonough, Truxton, Whipple, Worden, Blakeley, DeLong, Stockton, Strigham, Wilkes.

Foreign Ships.

ENGLAND.

Good Hope, 8 guns. Armored cruiser. Flagship of Rear Admiral Sir George Neville.
Argyl, 10 guns. Armored cruiser.
Hampshire, 10 guns. Armored cruiser.
Roxburgh, 10 guns. Armored cruiser.

GERMANY.

Roon, 14 guns. Armored cruiser. Flagship of Rear Admiral Zimmerman.
Bremen, 10 guns. Protected cruiser.

FRANCE.

Victor Hugo, 20 guns. Armored cruiser. Flagship of Rear Admiral Thierey.
Kleber, 12 guns. Armored cruiser.

JAPAN.

Tsukuba, 16 guns. Armored cruiser. Flagship of Vice-Admiral Ijuin.
Chitose, 12 guns. Protected cruiser.

ITALY.

Varese, 17 guns. Armored cruiser. Flagship of Rear Admiral Duke D'Abruzzi.
Etruria, 10 guns. Protected cruiser.

BRAZIL.

Riachuel, 10 guns. Third-class battleship. **Flagship** of Rear Admiral Duarte Huet de Barcellar.

CHILI.

Tamoyo, 2 guns. Cruiser.

PORTUGAL.

Don Carlos, 12 guns. Protected **cruiser.**

AUSTRIA.

Sant George, 11 guns. Armored **cruiser.**
Aspern, 8 guns. Protected cruiser.

SWEDEN.

Fylgia, 8 guns. Cruiser. Flagship of His Highness Prince Wilhelm.

ARGENTINE.

Presidente Sarmiento, 4 guns. Training ship.
Zenteno, 8 guns. Cruiser.

The battleships carry from six to eight hundred men each, the foreign boats usually having a larger crew than those of the American navy.

This magnificent spectacle is a sight that will live long in the memory of all who are fortunate enough to visit the Jamestown Exposition. It forms an impressive picture of fighting strength that will long be remembered in naval circles as the greatest gathering of warships in the history of the American nation and probably of the world.

PART III.

GENERAL ITINERARY.

The first important point to remember is that the Exposition site is on the shore of Hampton Roads, thirty minutes' ride by electric car from the city of Norfolk, and that Jamestown is merely an uninhabited island in the James River, forty miles from Norfolk.

For convenience, every visitor should also remember that Norfolk is the most accessible point to the Exposition and that many of the more historic places of interest can be reached from this city in from one to three hours. If possible, tourists should endeavor to return home by a different route, and a few suggestions are offered with this end in view.

New York to Norfolk.—By **Rail:** Via Philadelphia to Cape Charles. Boat from this point to Norfolk. **By Boat:** Distance 325 miles. Leaving New York by Old Dominion Line, at 3 p. m., boat reaches Norfolk at ten thirty the next morning. The itinerary for the return trip may of course be reversed. **Return** may be made by boat to Baltimore or Washington and from there to New York by rail.

Boston to Norfolk.—By **Boat:** Direct to Norfolk, or boat or rail to New York, and from there by rail via Philadelphia as given above.

Pittsburg and Western Points.—From Pittsburg by the B. & O. or from Harrisburg by the Pennsylvania, the tourist can proceed to Norfolk via Washington, Richmond and Petersburg. A stop-over should be made at each of these cities. The return trip may

be made by boat to Cape Charles and by rail via
Philadelphia and west via Harrisburg; or from
Philadelphia to New York and west over one
of the northern roads. Boat can also be taken from
Norfolk direct to Richmond or Washington. Boat
leaves Norfolk 6 p. m., arrives at Washington early
the next morning.

Southern Points.—Steamer connections between Norfolk and all important Atlantic ports. Rail connections via Raleigh, Chattanooga or Louisville.

Automobile Route.—The Annual Tour of the American Automobile Association will be to the Jamestown Exposition. **Route** via Washington through the Shenandoah Valley, via Richmond and Fredericksburg to Norfolk. Distance 250 miles. Macadam road almost the entire distance. Antietam, Harper's Ferry and Fredericksburg battlefields are included on the trip.

AUTOMOBILE ROUTE.

Washington to Hagerstown.

(*Hotels located here.)

Dupont Circle.....	1.5	Braddock's Springs	49.0
Montrose	12.6	Braddock's	
Rockville	15.4	Heights*	49.9
Gaithersville	20.06	Middletown* (Bat-	
Clarksburg	29.00	tlefields)	52.8
Hyattstown	32.9	Boonsborough	60.3
Frederick* (Old Na-		Funkstown	68.2
tional Highway..	44.5	Hagerstown*	71.

Hagerstown-Winchester.

Mappans	8.4	Sharpsburg	16.1
Dilghenington	10.4	Antietam Station..	17.8
Battlefield of An-		Shepard's Town...	20.4
tietam	13.7	Hall Town........	29.0

Charlestown* (John Brown hanged here) 33.0

Gaylord (State line) 41.7
Berryville* 40.0
Winchester* (National Cemetery). 57.1

Winchester to Staunton.

Kernstown 4.2
Bartonsville 6.0
Stephen's City ... 7.8
Middletown 12.2
Strasburg* (2.1 miles to Fisher Hill battlefield). 18.9
Tom's Brook 24.6
Mauretown 26.0
Triplet 29.0
Woodstock* 30.2
Taylor Town 35.0
Edinburgh 36.0
Hawkins Town ... 40.9

Mt. Jackson (Confederate monument) 42.6
Newmarket* (Luray cave 14 miles east) 50.5
Mauzy 57.8
Melrose 63.4
Harrisonburg* 68.4
Mt. Crawford* ... 76.1
Burke Town 78.9
Mt. Sidney 83.9
Verona 88.3
Staunton* (Nat'l Cemetery) 94.2

Staunton to Richmond.

Brand 3.0
Fishersville 6.5
Waynesboro 11.4
Basic City* (summer resort) 12.0
Spring (C. & O tunnel) 15.5
Afton* (summer resort) 16.4
Hillsbury 23.9
Brownsville 25.4

Mechum 28.2
Ivy 31.3
Woods Station ... 34.8
University of Virginia 37.4
Charlottesville* ... 38.4
Hunters' Hall 42.5
Shadwell 42.9
Boyd's Tavern ... 48.6
Zion 54.6
Trices 58.9

Driggsville 59.5
Moccassin Gap 67.7
Shannon Hill 70.1
East Leak 78.0
Gum Springs 82.0
Sandy Hook 84.0

Goochland Court
  House 89.6
State Farm 93.3
Issequena 96.5
Sabot 100.0
Manakin 102.9
Richmond* 118.6

Richmond to Norfolk.

Manchester 1.0
Petersburg* 21.6
Estes 29.7
Disputanta 36.8
Waverly* 48.5
Wakefield* 57.9
Ivor 66.7
Zuni 75.5
Windsor 83.3

Providence Church. 90.1
Kings Fork....... 90.7
Suffolk* 97.1
Stevers 100.5
Morris Fork 105.4
Drivers 107.2
Sholder Hill 109.1
Hodges Ferry 112.8
Norfolk* 119.6

Norfolk to Virginia Beach.

Oceana* 18.0

Virginia Beach* .. 21.2

Virginia Beach to Norfolk.

Oceana* 3.3
Rosemont 8.6

Norfolk 21.5

Norfolk to Richmond.

Portsmouth 0.4
Suffolk* 21.6
Windsor 36.3
Zuni 44.1
Wakefield* 60.7

Waverly* 70.3
Disputanta 81.8
Petersburg*· 95.7
Manchester 117.8
Richmond* 119.1

Richmond to Washington.

Fredericksburg*
  (Lee's Hill bat-
  tleground) 62.4
Falmouth 63.5
Aden 95.1

Bristow 100.4
Manassas (battle-
  field) 105.7
Fairfax C. H.*....119.9
Washington* 137.0

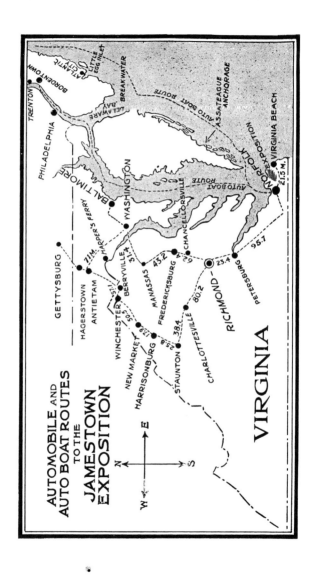

- .... . / .... .. -. -. - / .. ... / --- -. / ..-. --- .-. /
....- ----- ----- / .-.. .. .-.. .... / --- ..-. /
-... ..- -.-. .. -.. . -... / --. --- -.. --.. -.-. / - ---
... --- .-.. .. . / - .... . / -- --.- ... - . .-. -.-- /
--- ..-. / - .... . / .-- .- -- .... - .-. . -.. /
....- ----- ----- / .... . . -.. .-.. ...- / - .... . /
..- .. .. --- -. / ..-. --- -. ..- -- /
-.-. . - .- .-.. --- --- --. --. .